Voices In The Dreamtime

A Journey into the Self

H. Sydney Salt

InnerWorks Press
San Diego, California

Roy

Many blessings to

you —

Sydney Scott

Library of Congress Cataloguing-in-Publication Data
#97-093549

ISBN   0-9652596-2-5
1. Spiritual Journey
2. Shamanism
3. Self Help - Recovery

Cover Art & Illustration by Patti Fox
Photograph by Patina Rodgers

• • •

The author recognizes that we each create our own reality; that this creative process represents her personal journey, real and imagined.

Published by InnerWorks Press
P.O. Box 7422
San Diego, California   92167-0422

$14.95

TO MY READERS

In recent years, I have done a lot of talking. Talking to many people about my healing process, my philosophies and beliefs about living. I realized recently that they were "words on the wind". I was unwilling to capture them and put them into physical form.

It is my belief that we need to see our self expression given a creative form, that this gives us a sense of fulfillment that fills our soul.

I have always thought of myself as talker, a communicator of the spoken word. To think of myself as a communicator of the written word fills me with wonder. To have my thoughts and feelings put into physical, tangible form finally makes sense to me. I live in a physical world and my creativity must take this form also. It is time!

It is my hope that by sharing my inward process, you will be inspired on your path of self expression and whatever creative form it takes. We are all connected and affect each other's lives whether we wish to or not. It has become imperative for me to express what I know in a way that honours our collective spirit as well as my own.

For the past fourteen years, I have been on an intense journey of inward growth. I have learned things that seem so simple to me now but had never entered my consciousness before. These things are not new or earth shattering. Philosophers and healers have been expressing them for centuries. But they were new to me as I pieced them together and made them my expression for living. I saw these ancient truths in a different light, in the context of my own life. It became a matter of life and death as I stripped away my beliefs and masks that were passed down to me by religion, culture and my own family. Through creating sacred space and ceremony, I rediscovered my connectedness with the Earth and all living things. I came back into alignment with myself.

I have no doubt that I owe my healing to the qualities of the inner children both in adult and child form who have graced my life and shown me the way back home. I give my deepest gratitude and love to:

My darling daughter, Stefani Salt, who showed me my capacity for love and passion as she showed me hers.
Her kind father, Bob Salt, who gave me the protection and safety to uncover my woundedness.
My dear friend, Nancy Higgins, who accepted and nurtured me when I could not.
Her son, Willie Duvall, who taught me to go at my own pace in my own way.
My special friend, Raven Valencia, without whom I could not have healed my incest issues.
Her son, Corey Valencia, for showing me that although I believed myself to be broken, my spirit was not.
The twelve girl scouts whose troop I led for four years, who showed me my many expressive personalities.
My fellow traveler, Patti Fox (Pof) for sharing her creative kindred spirit and artistically expressing it in this book.
My cheerleader, Patti Serrano, for believing in my message and helping me put it into book form.
My intuitive editor, Christy Johnson, for being so gentle with my creative spirit, knowing when to edit and when to not.
My "blood brother", Karl Pennington, without whose computer expertise I would be lost.
My wise woman friend, Billie Delawie, for her encouragement and support in leading the way back home first.
Most of all, I owe my life to my own many inner children who found countless ways to survive their harsh world and yet, remained loyal in showing me the way back to wholeness..

I invite you to join me in this self expressive dance of life, nourishing ourselves with the wisdom of our life experiences as we transition into a new place of being.

* * * * * *

This book is dedicated to the feminine spirit in all of us and the masculine principle which manifests it.

Remember the magic!

1

I saw him squatting by the fire. His weathered face a dirty black, against the dark Australian night. Shadows danced across the creases of his face in the firelight. He looked very old and just a little scary. He had something white wiggling between his fingers. He was picking away at it, putting it to his teeth and making loud sucking noises. The Aborigines call it a witchety grub and it is considered a delicacy in the Outback. I watched quietly for some time, until I could wait no longer and approached the fire illuminating myself to his vision.

"What took you so long? You be waiting some time before you got up nerve to join me," he said without raising his eyes.

He was right, of course. I looked down at him, surprised he had felt my presence. And then mad at myself for my naivety. Of course, this man knew things. He knew the magic that others couldn't see. He didn't have to use his eyes.

His name is Namajira and he had come to me in a vision a couple of months before. I had gathered with some friends to make a rattle for ceremony, ritual and play. In my dreamtime, I had walked up to a cave opening nestled into the side of a hill. As I stood at the entrance, I saw a path going back into the cave and had hesitantly crept forward following its downward spiral until I reached a room where Namajira had stood. He asked the same question then, as he asked now, and then proceeded to tell me how to make my rattle.

"You make snake," he said, "and put rabbit on it."

As I have never taken anyone's advice without first understanding the meaning, I asked him why. "Snake symbolize shedding many skins; to be raw and new again. Rabbit, he be fear. Snake eat fear. It's good, yeh?"

"Yes," I said, "that is good". For so long, I have been afraid. Afraid of things I couldn't even recognize or necessarily articulate. Yes, it felt good to think that my fear could be eaten away.

"What else?" I asked.

"Remember the magic," he said. "You forgot the magic. Tis time to open door again. You be afraid for long time to enter magic place within your soul, but you do it now. Yea, you ready and I help." With those few words, he was gone and I was alone in the cave.

I came back to that room where my friends were, knowing I had begun yet another journey into the unknown. This time I was excited because I knew I wouldn't be alone. I had a teacher.

For the past fourteen years I have been on a journey of inner healing. For most of that time, I felt alone and isolated, occasionally gathering together with other seekers of truth, but always feeling that my path was one I must walk alone. It felt good to know that I was no longer alone and that perhaps, I never had been.

. . . . . .

As I gazed into the fire he spoke again, bringing me back to the present. "It's time to bring the magic to others, you know. You be procrastinating long enough." He stared long and hard into my eyes until I looked away in shame.

"I can't!" I said, "I don't know how. It's too hard to even think about. Namajira, what I know is so simple. People won't believe me. They don't want to know how much we complicate our lives and how simple it can really be. I can't do it!" I agonized. "You ask too much."

"This be your place, child, your place in the whole wide world. You must speak your truth," he assured me. "There are many who will not hear, but for those who do, you help bring them back into the family. Yea, tis important job you do. Do not deny your place in our world, it stop others from joining us."

I knew he was right, but even now as I write these words, I am filled with a certain sadness. I can no longer escape what I know and keep the secrets to myself. They are meant to be shared and I am supposed to lend my voice with others to speak the truth... my truth.

I'm also in conflict with myself for being the kind of person I have become. I want to blend in. I want to complain without taking action. I want to be a victim feeling hopeless and helpless to make changes within my world. But I know deep down in my heart, this is not the person I am. I cannot live with complacency any longer. I can no longer sit silently while something burns and churns within me to speak.

"Namajira, I honestly don't know where to begin," I admitted.

"You already begun, child, you live life in good spirit. As my brothers on Turtle Island say, 'you walk your talk'. It be where we all must start to change our world."

"But they don't want to do the work that makes it happen." I whined. "People already have the knowledge, but they are not committed to living it. Namajira, you can't make people listen when they don't want to hear and you can't make people do things if they are not motivated to do so."

"It is so, child, but you must share from your heart, not to change them, but to change yourself. This be their motivation and inspiration, to see it working in your life. It be up to them to find their path, just as you found yours. Many people share their story with you so that you could find your story, yes? You add your colour to great painting of life. Spirit, in fact, waiting for you."

He was right. I have felt for some time that it was time to tell my story, but I have not known where to begin.

First we must
separate to
come together.

2

"Where are we going?" I ask with intrepidation.

"Into the dreamtime," he replies with firm intent.

We are standing at the edge of a wide, windswept plain, surrounded by red sand with clumps of straggly bushes, randomly spaced across the horizon. There is no sign of human or creature habitation for miles and miles. Far off in the distance, I could see a lone ghost-gum tree standing starkly against the turquoise, cloud-clotted sky. The colours stand out in sharp contrast; the red earth, the blue sky and the black skin of my friend, Namajira.

"I can't go, I am not prepared, I'm not ready, I don't know what to do! I'm so scared to let go of what seems real to me in this land," I stutter. "You can't ask me to."

He murmurs gently in my ear. "Take my hand, child, we will enter the dreamtime together."

With that soft command, I close my eyes and hold out my hand, as a fierce wind swirls around me, lifting me off the ground. I can't see Namajira, but I hold fiercly onto his hand, trying hard to believe that I will be alright. I hear the sound of birds and a long, low whirring noise which grow louder and louder until it is all I can hear. It feels as though I'm somehow being cleansed and I finally relax into the sounds flowing into and out of my head.

When I open my eyes, I'm lying on the sand and listening to the sound of ocean waves washing onto the shore. I hear everything so vividly; the water rolling and forming its waves as it tumbles onto the sand, the seagulls squawking their raucous cries as they declare their territory on the beach. I can even hear the sand crabs scratching and digging into the harsh particles of sand. Namajira is nowhere to be found as I quickly scan the beach. I am alone except for a distant and strange hum I hear behind me.

I focus on the humming as it becomes louder and louder. Once again I feel myself being propelled along, following the sound which has evolved into a continuous thump of a heartbeat, like a giant drum being pounded.

As I walk toward some bushes away from the

shoreline, I glance up feeling the sprinkle of rain spattering my head and shoulders. Yet, as I enter into the jungle-like terrain, I'm protected from the onslaught as it begins to pour down. It seems like only moments of following a haphazard trail before I part some leaves and I am looking into a clearing. I see a number of men sitting on their haunches around a large, crackling fire. The rain has stopped. In fact, I see no evidence that it has rained at all. The men appear dry, as is the ground they squat on. The fire is dancing and sparking as though it has been burning for hours. The low whirring sound is coming out of a long hollow tube-like instrument which I recognize as a didjeridoo. It calls me closer to the fire.

I hear the rattle sound of a snake, the clicking of sticks, the steady beat of a drum, as they all blend together in an eerie cacophony of magical sounds. African, aboriginal, asian and american native tribal sounds blending together, yet each distinguished by their own unique melody within the continuing strand of sound and silence. I am lost in a world of sound. Before me stands Namajira, who is welcoming me to the circle, his faint smile calming my nervous spirit. Where am I going? What am I doing? It doesn't matter. I am being pulled into the circle and into the earth. I become oblivious to the men around me. I am alone as I have been many times before. And I hear the creation of sacred space as a voice speaks:

"Dingo Dog dreaming to the West." These words calling me to be wild, instinctual. A message of loyalty and truth to myself and others.

"Water Buffalo dreaming to the North." Telling me to honour all living things. To trust in my world and honour my place in it, as I can do for others.

"Kangaroo dreaming to the South." Speaks of leaping forward with joy and hope. Becoming the child of nature's way, feeling the safety of the womb that Mother Earth creates for us to be nurtured and nourished.

"Dolphin dreaming to the East." Inviting me to play and breathe in life's magic. The words reminding me it is time to honour Great Spirit, and my own Spirit, by becoming the creator.

From out of the smoke, one man stands and speaks quietly to the circle. "Our world is changing, but we must go back to find strength. Once more, we must go back to the ritual and ceremony of the land to discover our connectedness. Our connection to ourselves is discovered through our relationship to the earth and all living things. We know this, but it has been forgotten by others." He lowers his head, closing his eyes. Then continues.

"We have forgotten what we can change and what we cannot. Our lives must become simple again through following the earth's energy. It is so simple and yet, so hard for many to do. It is time to teach others how, for they are ready to listen now." He paused, then continued.

"They have lost their way through walls of concrete some call technology and isolation of their spirit. They forget we are all the same in Spirit." He beats his chest with one fist, "Our blood, our bones, our organs are the same, only our outsides are different. Our skin colour, this we cannot change - nor are we meant to - for it expresses our individuality. It is good to remember how we fit together to make a painting of life."

"Yeh, it is time to unite the colours of humanity," he smiles, continuing. "Our time, brothers, has come again, to teach the way to pierce the veils of illusion and distrust. To break away once more, into ourselves, and collect our hidden memories. Time now to share the secrets of being in our Earth world."

As he sits down, the sounds become louder and the drum beat more intense, as each man answers the call to the challenge that has been laid down.

I look around in wonder, not daring to breathe or make a sudden move for fear of breaking the spell that has been cast around me. I know his words. I hear his truth. I have lived it many times before. I'm living it again now. It was how I got here. Yet, this time it is different. My skin is the only white skin present in the circle, my gender the only one of its kind. I wonder why I am part of this circle. It seems, as it has many times in the past, that I don't fit. Why am I here?

As if in response to my question, a slim, proud-looking man stands up. With his spear pointing toward me, he speaks.

"You are here, woman, because we called you. You have walked the path of many of us here, in times gone past, and you have remembered the essence of those lives. You are the integration of all our people and we have chosen you to speak for us in the outside world. In your woman form, people will receive your message of attunement to Spirit and your ability to respond through trusting the magic and mystery of life. Your male and female shields are in balance and you will be heard by those who are ready to hear your story."

I pondered these words. My experiences had taught me that I was too intense, too dramatic. I didn't think anyone would want to listen. Time clicked back as I remembered an age when I didn't want to listen.

It was my first conscious wakeup call. I had caught a cold which had grown progressively worse until the doctors couldn't give an accurate diagnosis and named it pneumonia. I was taking large doses of medicine to cure me, but all it seemed to do was make me sicker. One night I was in yet another fitful sleep when I was jerked awake by a voice saying, "There is another way, find another way." I had known instantly that I needed to explore alternative healing forms. That singular voice led me toward a series of conscious actions and alternative practices that brought me back to wholeness. But I had to get to the bottom of my physical and emotional well before I could listen to "the knowing" and respond.

"White woman, you, and leaders like you, have paved the way for others. It is no longer a choice you make, you must continue to follow your path. It is your way," said a deep voice through the smoke.

It was true. Once I had made the commitment to my healing process, there was no turning back and no stopping the momentum. I was caught in the flow of eternal energy coursing through my body, and as much as I resisted, I could not stop it, nor did I really want to. I wanted to find my spirit and put the pieces of my being back together. It became my quest and later, much later, my conquest.

The didjeridoo bellowed into the silence of the night. The steady pound of the drum matched my heartbeat as I strained to listen to my spirit. Out of the sounds of silence came a haunting melody. Someone was singing.

> *"Take me home*
> *For I am weary of being alone.*
> *Take me back to my family where I belong.*
> *It's been so long,*
> *I've forgotten how it feels to be me and free.*
> *Take me home."*

I cannot see who is singing. The song feels like it is coming through my heart. I wonder, "Is this circle my family? Is this Earth my home?" I am most at home in nature now, but there was a time that it frightened me.

I was afraid of its unpredictability and the lack of real protection I felt. I had experienced this feeling before as a child within the confines of my home and family. That feeling of being vulnerable to the unpredictable and capricious moods of my parents. There was no protection then, and no place to hide. Just endure and survive. How ironic it is that it all came down to that basic mode. Nature's gift was to show me what I needed to heal and to ask for more than mere endurance and survival. It's never been enough for me to be content with the way things are. There had to be more; there had to be answers, and I was determined to find them out for myself. Nature paved the way.

. . . . . .

Once I was hiking the hills amongst the red rocks of Sedona, Arizona. It was February and cold and wet. I wanted to hike Bell Rock, a bell-shaped monolith not far out of town. Early that morning, I had set out by myself with a heavy jacket and a hat for protection against the elements. The air was cool to my face and the rain, light and misty, a little more than invigorating. I wound my way around and up the rock's face until I reached a point where I could see for miles. The rain became a little heavier but still not terribly uncomfortable. I sat down on the rock next to a tree offering a little protection from the wind and drank in the beauty of the scene. The colours surrounding me were magnificent. The dark rust red of the rocks, the green of the occasional shrub, and the whistling pine trees in the distance, all complemented the steel gray of the sky with its patches of blue far off on the horizon. In spite of the mild discomfort afforded me by the weather, I felt a certain sense of accomplishment for having braved the elements and conquered the rock.

I remember tilting my face to the sky, allowing the rain to gently wash away my mask of self-deception and doubt. I was at peace. Later, as I headed back down the rock, I became afraid and a prickly sense of panic seized me. I couldn't find the same path down that I had taken up. I looked around wildly trying to find something familiar that I could use as a starting point. But the rain was running down the rocks hard now, and the mists, much thicker, were making it difficult to see very far in front of me. I was alone and frightened.

I knew I couldn't stay there because no one would come looking for me. I had to find my way back down. I stood there, tears of frustration and anger mixing with the heavy rain. And then I heard, "Follow the water line. It will lead you home." Looking around I saw that the water was running down in rivulets over the rocks and had made channels from previous rains. I began to follow one channel down until it dropped abruptly off a ledge. I looked around again, for another one and followed it to its conclusion. I continued to follow these waterways until, at last, I found myself at the bottom of the rocks and near my car. Soaking wet from rain and tears, I gratefully thanked my spirit guides and Mother Earth for getting me down off the mountain and teaching me my lessons.

I learnt many things that day. I learnt to be still. To listen and trust that a message would be given if I were open to receiving it. I learnt that if I was to continue growing, then I must take a different path down than I had taken up, and that it was almost impossible to retrace my steps, and perhaps, a waste of energy.

Most significant, I learnt to follow the water to return home. I interpreted this many ways that day both in a physical way and in an emotional context. I had been far removed from my feelings, depending instead on logic and mental reasoning to make sense out of my life. But, it was returning to my emotions and finding my spirit that carried me home. It has been my path ever since.

. . . . . .

Once more, my attention is brought back to the fire circle. A short, plump figure with a large disk placed through his lower lip rises to speak. He hesitates, then speaks deliberately.

"First we must separate to come together. You cannot find yourself when you are joined to others. The break must occur so that you will see where you end and another begins. Otherwise your experience becomes theirs, their path becomes yours and there is great confusion. Many times I became attached to someone's experience, trying to find the common thread to our humaness, but often I lost myself."

As he sat down, I thought of the time when I had to make a break from a dear friend. I was struggling. It was not the first time in a relationship where I felt the time had come to disconnect our energies. While the friendship had been supportive for our growth, it was beginning to choke off the new development which occurred as we each continued to do our individual work.

I had felt sad. Somehow, it was not right to grow apart and move in another direction. I had done this with many relationships. Each time blaming myself for not being able to sustain the relationship when, in fact, not recognizing that it was a natural part of growth. I began to see that every child must do this with his or her parent. It is not that the connection must be severed, but disconnected, so that the energy we draw upon becomes our own and not that of the other person. As with the birth of a child, the umbilical cord must be cut from the mother. Both mother and child are still connected, but the child must find another source from which to draw her energy and nourishment, eventually finding her own source as she reaches maturity.

Throughout my healing process, I saw that I was constantly growing and becoming independent from others, although I still felt connected in spirit. The essence and challenge of my relationships, whether it was with a person, animal or the earth, was to find my own spirit and come into a place of integration with those parts of me that I had denied or had been denied me by others. Every interaction I have gives me a precious opportunity to find a piece of the puzzle, my puzzle. Whether the interactions have been long or short term, I have felt enormously rewarded by these gifts of growth.

. . . . . .

Once, I was hiking with a friend. We had

decided to find our way to the top of a high cliff overlooking a beautiful valley. Together, we started our climb, gently meandering across a gradual slope, keeping each other in sight. The way soon became more difficult and we both stopped frequently, hesitating to see which way would be the safest and easiest for both of us. It soon became apparent that my friend's sense of ease and safety was different from mine. Our body types alone pointed out this difference. He was tall and lanky while I am short and solid. We needed to separate and find our own way up the cliffs using our own particular style of movement and perceptions. I remember feeling a weight drop from my shoulders as I realized what a responsibility it was to guide someone else on a path I had chosen for myself. I didn't like being followed nor did I feel comfortable following someone else. I wanted to be free to find my own path and allow my friend to find his. We both found our way to the top feeling exhilarated and proud of our individual accomplishment. We had separated to come together.

. . . . . .

My attention is slowly brought to the fire circle. Namajira looks over at me, nodding. He is looking past me, through me, to a point beyond my head. Suddenly, he leaps into the air. I see for the first time that his face and body are marked with white clay. His ghostlike presence stands above the flames of the fire. One arm is by his side and the other, held high above his head, clutches a spear.

I hold my breath. I feel my heart beat frantically in my chest. With each beat of the drum, he jabs the air, attacking and retreating to an ancient rhythm that only he hears. His body jerks and contorts until it becomes a blur of light dancing across the fire circle. I am held spellbound as my body answers the call of his beckoning dance. In my hand is a rattle, my snake rattle made with my friends some months ago. I look down to see that I am naked. My mind is numb, without reasoning.

Suddenly I am jangled out of my questions by a loud piercing scream. Namajira leaps across the fire to join me. My heart feels as though it jumped into the air with him. As much as I try to understand what is happening, nothing makes sense. The men around the fire begin to chant in short, staccato sounds, slowly at first, then building into a crescendo of echoes that remove all rational thought from my mind.

Namajira advances toward me carrying a

clay bowl. Inside the bowl, there are four compartments, each holding a different colour of wet and sticky clay. My body tenses as two men advance toward me pulling me to my feet. They stand beside me, one holding my arms, the other my legs. I am on the edge of fear, and yet, I know I am safe. So I do not struggle, but surrender to the drama unfolding around me. Three more men approach us and stand beside Namajira. With his first and middle fingers, my teacher dips into the bowl extracting some white clay, smearing it onto my left arm in a strange zig-zag design.

"This is to honour our brothers of the white skin. It is a symbol of the renewal of their energy. Like lightning, they must be struck with intensity to change their destructive thought patterns." Namajira speaks with passionate intention.

As he finishes, he passes the bowl to the man on his left. This man is tall and wiry with an ugly scar crossing his cheek. His face looks angry, his whole demeanour aggressive, as I shrink from his touch. Yet when he does touch me, it is as though a feather grazed my arm.

"With this dark brown clay, I honour the black men whose time has come to show compassion for themselves and recreate their ritual of brotherhood in a gentler way." His eyes are full of understanding as he smears wriggly marks on my other arm before passing the bowl to the third man.

"I honour the spirit of the red man. His way has been long and sorrowful. His spirit almost crushed beneath the hand of man's greed and need for dominion over the land and its people. May he be honoured for his suffering and his way of living on this earth." As he spoke, this gentle and grave man marks my leg with an upward spiral of red clay.

The fourth man approaches quietly, painting my remaining naked leg with dots and long lines drawn with yellow clay.

"For our brothers of the yellow skin, I honour his sense of beauty and his path of flowing with the way of balance in all things."

All four men step back into the circle as I stand gazing dazedly into the fire. From behind me, I catch the haunting sound of a wooden flute as it plays its song of yearning and despair, love and hope. I sway gently to the music, bending to the melody as I close my eyes and let my body express its longing for oneness among the people of our earth.

Follow
the
energy.

3

"Come back, child, come back." Namajira is sitting beside me, gently touching my brow. My head is spinning with vivid colours swirling together in a rainbow spiral. I don't want to open my eyes. My heart feels heavy, my body sore. I am lying on the red earth where we first stood when Namajira took my hand to lead me into the dreamtime. I look down at my body and see faint tracings of mud and clay on my arms and legs.

"It was real, wasn't it, Namajira? I was there at the council fires."

"We journey long time together. You meet my brothers. We did ceremony with you. Yes, you there."

"But why did you leave me on the beach? I felt lost and abandoned. I didn't know what to do."

"That be idea, woman-child. You must find your own way to the circle, use instincts and desire to find your way. I only take you so far, the rest up to you. You did well!" Namajira beams down at me.

"Everything in this whole world be co-creation, you know. You do your part, I do mine. We join together to create something greater than original thought, or impulse. You know this by now. Yes?"

"Yes," I answer, "but what has been hard for me, Namajira, is finding out what I want to do and bringing that into creation. For many years, I had to learn just how to survive my world. I made a choice based on someone else's input. Then, I either rebelled or conformed. Before, there was a wall of resistance that I bounced off. Now there is a void. How do you fuel the void and create something out of nothing?" I hold my breath as I wait his wise words.

"It be sometimes hard to create understanding where there be no basis of experience. That be where trust come in. To stay in void uncomfortable. Many try to fill empty feeling with food, friends, work, drugs and yes, sex. You call them stimulants, some say become addictions. But this not be answer, space must be emptied to allow light to enter. When you clean out closet, it allows more space for new things to be put in, yeh? So it is with our bodies.

We must clean out our closets, so to speak. Heh, heh! It's funny, yeh?" We smile at one another.

"But tis true," he explains. "When we do this, light shines in on void and we find not void at all, but myriad of ideas and thoughts waiting to be acted upon. Which one you choose depends on excitement you feel toward it. If you pick puppy from a litter, one stands out and draws itself to you. That be one you respond to. There be no reasoning, just simple attraction, mostly, heart connection, too."

"But I want to make sense of my choices!" I demand. "Yet when I do, I end up going against my original idea. I cut off the energy before it has a chance to be brought into form. I know now that I cut off the desire for it in the first place because as a child I was taught it was wrong to want something without a good reason. Now I get confused as to what is the right choice because nothing has that excitement attached to it any more."

Suddenly, I feel my mood changing to sadness. "Sometimes, I think it was easier when I was told what was the right choice. It's hard taking responsibility for my choices now because I feel the decision could be made either way and that there is no wrong direction to pursue."

"You be right, child. There be no wrong choice. In the end, all paths lead to greater learning and understanding. But Spirit want to make it easy on you. Why you take hard way when you can do what you like, what excites you? What happened at fire ceremony? Did you take hard way?"

"Well, it depends how you look at it. I was terrified. I had no idea what was happening, but it seemed easier to surrender and let go of trying to make sense out of everything than fight it. Besides," I smile shyly, "I was intensely curious."

"Ahh, so you trust and let go. You chose straight away path even though it not look easy." He smiles back, "Maybe it intrigue you?"

"Yes, I did trust and let go," I say in wonder. "I really did. And, Namajira, I didn't get hurt either. I was afraid I'd get hurt somehow."

"See! Spirit has plan for you. You gave up fighting him. Always follow energy that is present. It is quickest way to understanding. Don't think. Do! Spirit presents you with learning. Respond!"

"So, why was I at the council fire, Namajira? I don't feel I have any idea what I'm doing. Everything is so confusing. I don't know how to make sense out of my life right now."

"What be troubling you, child?"

I take a deep breath and begin. "In the past, I have felt a strong sense of purpose to my life. As a teenager, I couldn't wait to get a job and leave home to explore my world. I wanted to experience it all; I loved traveling to far away places and meeting new and different people. I couldn't wait to fall in love. When I did meet my special mate, life was still an exciting adventure as I pushed forward into making a business career for myself." I look sideways at Namajira to see if I still have his attention and continue.

"The greatest achievement of my life came when I gave birth to my daughter. From that moment on, my life expanded into a bewildering world of intense feelings. As I slowly, many times painfully, began nurturing this wonderful miracle of life that had graced my world, I began to see that I didn't know how to take care of her. I saw that the world around me was fraught with dangers that I wanted to protect my daughter from experiencing. And perhaps what was most frightening, I began to see that her greatest danger was from me and the many unconscious acts and beliefs I was thrusting upon her. It became my commitment to make her world a kinder and gentler place than I had known, and I began with me."

Namajira shifted his gaze from the horizon to

me and slowly nodded his head. It gave me confidence to continue.

"Namajira, I didn't know when I began my journey of inner healing how great my pain would be. I didn't know that I would tear away every mask I wore to protect myself. I would examine every belief I had grown up with, breaking down the walls, restructuring the foundation of my very existence, to rebuild a new way of being. I owe my life, as it is now, to my daughter. In a sense, it was she who gave birth to me. It is a gift I can never repay because she gave me back my life. A life now filled with love and compassion, not just for myself, but for others, too. I want to share this precious gift of life that my daughter gave me and I don't know how. That is where my confusion lies. How do I do this, Namajira?" I hung my head, feeling relief that I had finally put into words what had been worrying me for the past year.

"You know I don't have answer for you, child. It is something you must discover for yourself. Like you did with everything else in your life. You be good at finding and listening to only you for your healing. Why you want me to tell you now. You won't listen anyhow."

"Yes, I will." I cried. "I'm ready now to hear other people's wisdom.

To listen to their story of success."

"OK to listen, yes, but still not your path. You must find your own."

"I can't. I've tried. I'm tired of doing all the work alone. I want someone to help me now." I knew I was sounding like a petulant child, but I couldn't help it. Just this once I wanted a parent to tell me where to go. Then I'd be on my way. I'd run out of having a sense of purpose for my being here on this planet and I needed answers now.

I look up to take note of my surroundings and see the sharp desolation of the desert. It matches my spirit. Namajira is looking off into the distance and I watch his proud profile, trying to gauge his reaction to my confession. His forehead is large, his head tilted up. A gentle breeze ruffles his straggly black-gray beard. His face gives nothing away. I know he holds much sorrow in his heart. He had watched his people lose their spirit in the face of the white settlers of Australia. Some had turned to the white man's vice of alcohol to numb the despair of losing their way, others had retreated further into the outback turning away from the white man's influence and desecration of their sacred lands. Both acts, isolated themselves from the tribe. Their spirits were disconnected now where once they had been whole. Their connection to the earth was scattered and fragmented. They had lost or hidden most of their ritual and ceremony because of the white man's domination over their land and their attempt to "civilize the Aborigine."

It had not been easy for Namajira to witness and participate in his own spiritual death and that of his people. He told me once that he had failed as a leader of his people, as he was forced to watch the disintegration of a way of life that had survived for thousands of years. He carried a heavy burden, and yet, he carried it with a resignation and acceptance of what life had presented him.

It never occurs to me to feel sorry for Namajira. I feel only respect and wonder at how magnificently he holds himself. He seems to know himself and his purpose in life. I want so much for him to tell me mine. But he remains silent, only offering me his compassionate eyes of understanding.

Be patient with
yourself ...

for you are
in the
process
of
learning and
discovery.

4

I am alone! My time with Namajira is both exhilarating and bewildering. I enjoy exploring into barely glimpsed territories of my mind and spirit with someone by my side. But I feel I am no closer to understanding what it is I'm supposed to do with my life. I'm so frustrated and confused! How can I know so much and not be able to put it into form to share with others? What am I so afraid of?

Yet, I know I am already "walking my talk" as Namajira told me. So many times I tell my friends that life is a process, that each day is a completion in itself. But I continually doubt my own words. I know life has no goal, simply the moment-by-moment living which leads to a sense of achievement. For me, that achievement is rarely what I planned. And I only recognize it as such after I have put some perspective and distance to it.

"Trust!" Namajira says, but I find it so difficult! Sometimes I see a vision of where I want to be and yet, I can't find the way to get there. Sometimes the vision changes and I get confused as to what choice I should make. When I choose a path and try to make it happen, it feels forced and the way becomes hard. If, as Namajira says, "It is already in place," then surely all I must do is allow the steps to reveal themselves and take them one-by-one. In my heart I know this to be true, but to trust and believe it is to sit in the void. I was taught that to be still is to be lazy and unproductive. I must do something, anything, to keep moving. But at times, I do see a river of energetic movement and information already flowing through my life. Sometimes I must be still to find it. Yes, the river takes me where I need to go, but not always where I expect to go.

I tend to be rigid in a fluid world. I want to control my life so that I won't get hurt. But I get hurt anyway. So why do I try to control it in the first place? Namajira says, "Surrender to the energy present". But that means I must trust. "Trust what?" I've asked. Trust that there is a purpose to every movement and every living thing; that there is a Great Spirit that connects us all? I believe this, intellectually at least. Trust that each thing has its purpose whether it be a plant, an animal, a season or a human and together we grow and spiral our way back to the Source, to God?

Yes, I know this! But do I trust that the way back is a journey of grace, accepting that I will be provided with what I need to evolve and integrate my spirit with others? This is the hardest part. It means to surrender my will, my fighting spirit that has kept me alive through my most difficult challenges and to trust God. I'm afraid to do this! The "God" I grew up believing in was not there for me. It hurt to trust before. Will it be different this time? And why?

I believe I know the answers now. I have tested my truth against the reality of others. I have taken responsibility for my past experiences and found the lost children inside me. I've reclaimed my fragmented spirit. I've collected the painful unacknowledged feelings and come to a place of resolution with them. I've found out who I am and hold a place of love and acceptance for all that I was - a wounded, frightened child who only wanted love and acceptance and to give the same to others.

So why do I still feel so sad, unloved and afraid to start this new adventure called living? For the first time in my life, I am walking as a whole person. My heart hurts and bursts at the same time, my tears are mingled with joy and pain. I am filled with compassion and grief for every living thing and I'm not sure I can live in this world where there is so much shame and denial of these feelings inside me.

It is easy to play scenes out in my mind, but never put them into physical form. I've done this for so long I'm not sure I know how to shift gears and create a new physical reality. I realize that I've been living a mental reality and it has stifled the physical expression of my dreams.

My dreams are precious to me now. I was afraid to reveal them for fear of having them taken away. But now, when I weigh the option of having them spin around in my head, going nowhere, I feel compelled to risk that fear.

My dream is to share my experiences with others so that together we can break down our walls of isolation and protection. I want to reveal my spirit to you so that you can know me and see that we are one. No matter what your shape, your colour, your outside experiences, I want to recognize the real you and I want you to do the same for me. I don't think we can do this if I don't show you my softness, as well as, my strengths. In fact, it is my softness, my woundedness that is my strength and what draws you to me. It is my true spirit, not the facade I have built around me to protect it.

Perhaps it is the feminine spirit. I'm not sure. When I try to define it as male and female spirit, I get confused. I sense it is all the same. In my attempt to understand my world I have separated the pieces that make it whole. In the world I grew up in, everything was divided into twos; black and white, good and bad, love and hate, soft and hard. I was forced to make a choice between the two sides. I can't do that anymore. Both sides are part of the whole and I can no longer separate one from the other without making one acceptable and one not. And that is not my reality now. I will not segregate parts of me any more.

I think my shame in revealing the whole me, has been based in the belief that to be emotional is weak and wrong. To express those feelings physically, like tears of sadness and joy, anger, letting others witness my emotions, fills me with shame. But If I am to break down my walls of isolation and protection, I must share my tears and fears as well as my laughter and joy. For they are all part of the whole me.

Perhaps what I am most ashamed of is my innocence. The childlike me, who does not know how to live comfortably in this world, but is willing to make mistakes and explore it, freely and safely. There is so much I do not know. But I am tired of learning from people who only share what I have done wrong and feel the need to fix me. I remember as a child my feelings of being unacceptable was almost overwhelming. Voices parroting, "You talk too much, your behaviour is inappropriate." Any simple self expression was held up to ridicule, punishment or criticism. Even today, when someone places themselves in a position of authority and superiority, I feel so worthless and flawed that it almost paralyzes any desire I have to manifest my dreams. I begin to believe that their experiences are the only valid ones. I accept their reality while I negate my own desire to follow the dream and vision I perceive for myself.

This, I can do no longer. My passion for my life compels me to place it in the circle of all life, honouring your reality and truth, but having the courage to tell you mine. This is my commitment to you and to myself.

Respect all living things...
for these
are the
teachers
of life,
through
these

you connect with
Great Spirit.

5

I am sitting beside a lake. The sun is shining although the air is cool. My back is resting against a tall oak-like tree with its large roots splayed up out of the earth, leaving pockets of space to imagine chairs and lounges gracefully placed around the tree. The lake is calm and matches my spirit. I am feeling a deep sense of peace and acceptance of where I am and who I am.

It has been a number of weeks since I last had contact with Namajira. I've been afraid. Afraid of losing myself in his world and not coming back to my reality. Now that I know I am to share my thoughts and process of living with you, my reader and fellow traveller, I am concerned that he might abandon me just as I had abandoned myself so many times before.

But I am ready to continue and I need to ask for his help and guidance. As I look out on the smooth surface of the lake, I take in a few deep breaths, cleansing my body from the inside out and feeling the roots underneath my buttocks as I anchor myself to the earth/tree. I reach inside my body with my mind and follow the line of my breath until I find my creative centre just below my navel. The image of a yellow-orange flower unfolds before my eyes and I feel secure and solid to call in my spirit teacher.

"Namajira, I am calling you. Will you come?" I whisper. He once told me that all I had to do was wish for his presence and he would appear, but I did not believe that it would happen. Instead I rely on him appearing to me when he wishes. Why should I believe that someone would come to me at the time I wanted them. In the physical world, this had not happened with my parents and friends so it has become hard to put faith into my spirit world and believe.

My old experiences belied this new reality. Gently, I open my eyes to see a tall, wiry and familiar figure standing in front of me. He is holding a spear with his head cocked to one side as if he were listening to my mind chatter and having trouble making sense out of it. "He wasn't the only one," I thought. And he smiled, hearing my thoughts.

"How be you, child? I have missed our time together. But I be watching you and waiting for your call."

I felt warmed by his words. I am, once more, back home. Something has shifted in me. I can feel it. There is more acceptance coming from my spirit. I feel safer being in this world and I feel confident that I can bridge back into my physical world when I need to. My spirit is calmed.

"I want to tell you about my dog, Cloud." I blurt out without any pretense at preamble.

"Ah, yes," he said as he positioned himself in a large pocket of the root-structured tree.

"I've been so sad. I had to put my dog to sleep, Namajira. I feel such remorse and such an incredible sense of loss. I think it was the right thing to do, but this feels so painful, I'm beginning to doubt my decision. And I want to distract myself from the pain I'm feeling."

"I understand, child. It be hard to walk through pain. Perhaps you be afraid you get stuck, not come out into light again."

"Yes, that is part of it. But I'm also afraid that I've made the wrong decision and that I will be punished for it. I don't want to face the judgement of my decision. I am already living with the consequences. I felt I did the best thing at the time, I don't want to hear that I should have done it differently. So I keep distracting myself so I don't have to examine my motives and feelings."

"But you don't, child. Just accept that you acted with the right intention. You not have to justify actions to yourself or anyone else either."

"But then, how do I know I did the right thing?"

"You learnt many things, did you not? Cloud's sickness and death cause you to walk your path more consciously, yeh? Animals give us gift of insight and growth. You know this, right? So tell me your story of your spirit keeper, Cloud. I will listen."

I took a deep breath and began slowly. "Cloud came to me when she was a pup, all round and fluffy. At the time I was married and she was supposed to be a Christmas present for us all, my husband, daughter and me.   But she was for me. She came into my life at a time when I was searching for some answers to my unease and unhappiness. She filled a place in me I didn't know was lacking, a place of love, loyalty and acceptance. She became my teacher in finding these things in myself."

"Over the years, we went on many adventures together. I took her to a dog training school where I first realized that there was a part of Cloud that was wild, free and totally untrainable.

This manifested in many ways, the simplest being that if she wanted to do something or go somewhere, nothing would stop her, not even the leash I had attached to her collar. She would break away to my cries of entreaty to come back and only return when she had finished her expedition. There appeared to be no remorse, just an acceptance that she had needed to pursue her goal, whatever it was at that moment."

"She taught me very early on in my training, that if I was angry with her and approached her, she would bare her teeth and attack me. If I came at her with love and acceptance, she was a willing partner in whatever I wanted to do with her. I learned that it wasn't my words or even my hand raised that provoked her but the energy I carried to her.

"Sometimes, with other people, she would begin "talking" to them until they came into themselves. Then she would saunter away. I learnt to recognize that these people were distracted, fragmented, and she was trying to bring them back into their bodies, to be fully present with their surroundings. I watched her teach others as she taught me. No one who came into her presence left untouched by her in some way."

"I learnt that when she came and sat beside

me, it was time to tune into myself and see where I needed to be loyal to myself. I found out that when she acted out some outrageous behaviour, there was a message for me to relate to in my life. It was she who gave me the kind of unconditional love and acceptance of my spirit that helped me reach back out to connect with people, the ones who had so hurt my spirit in the first place."

I fell silent, remembering.

"In the last couple of months, I felt her spirit move away from mine. I can't put a specific behaviour to it, just a feeling that she was moving in another direction that didn't include me. She began sleeping outside more often and only came in when we had friends visiting. We would take long walks in the canyon below our house, and she would wander off, but now she would come when I called her. I knew then that something had shifted in our relationship. She gradually stopped eating her food and drank very little water," tears welled up as I remembered.

"When I took her to the vet, he could find nothing wrong with her, but she continued to refuse food and water. On her last day on this earth I sat with her a long time asking for guidance. I realized that she had done her earthwalk with me and it was time for her to move back into spirit.

I didn't understand this with my mind, nothing made sense in a rational way, only my spirit knew. It was time for her to go and I had to help her. She, who had kept me anchored to this place called earth, was asking me to release her spirit."

"Namajira, I had never witnessed death before. I've always been frightened of it. But I knew I had to honour Cloud for the life that she gave me by witnessing her death. She died in my arms, gracefully and gently, with her head resting in my arms. I held her and sang to her spirit, praying that her spirit would rise swiftly to its new place of being. I knew when her heart stopped and I wailed at my loss. This beautiful creature had taught me how to find me, love myself and accept all of who I was, not just the parts that others wanted to accept and love in me. She held my broken spirit until I could make it whole. I will miss her so much. She sacrificed her spirit to show me I now had mine."

Namajira looked across the lake and back into my eyes. I saw compassion and sadness expressed in them and I felt a weight lift from my shoulders. I had shared my pain. It felt good not to shoulder it by myself and to have a witness to my grief and torment.

H. Sydney Salt

"Let us walk together, dear one. Let soft winds of nature's spirits sweep away your grief and gentle your heart. You do much honour to animal world and they be grateful, just as you grateful to them. Come feel their gratitude."

The lake was still calm, yet now I saw a gentle breeze whisper in the leaves of the trees. I felt my world, alive. A butterfly flit over the grass, looking for something to land on. It was orange and black, its wings very large. Namajira nudged my arm as together, we saw where it had landed. The flower was golden yellow like the image of my centre. I felt at peace. Finally.

Believe in yourself ...

For upon this rests
your ability to succeed.

6

It has been almost a year since I last had a conversation of any significance with my friend, Namajira. I lost my way and turned my back, not only on him, but on myself also. I felt I turned my back on my own desires and dreams. Now, I am asking for them back.

I am sensing that my time with Namajira is coming to a close, at least the way in which we come together. I see that part of his purpose of becoming present with me was to bring me into my own aspect of leadership, helping me to take responsibility for my place within the tribe, this community that I live in. I felt he wanted to bring forth my courage and belief in myself so that I could express my voice, my self expression in the world I had become so frightened of rejoining. It is finally happening, but not without the assistance of special earth people who helped to propel me into my place of inheritance. It is time to bring Namajira up-to-date.

As I call all of my energy and attention to be present, my body is vibrating and I am becoming increasingly uncomfortable with the feeling. I suspect that this discomfort is from being deeply rooted in my body, an exercise in consciousness I had not previously experienced before I started this creative process. It happens every time I sit down to write. I am frightened of this energy and I want to escape. I want to numb the feeling with food. Sometimes I get up and leave, anything to rid myself of the intensity and discomfort.

I don't fully understand it, although it has something to do with the creative energy also being a sexual energy, and to claim it is somehow bad. I'm terrified it will consume me, as it did when I was a child, when I would lose days at a time going someplace in my mind where the other parts of me didn't even know about. I do know that I was not mindfully present in my physical reality, and eventually lost gaps of memory throughout most of my childhood. Learning to split off my emotions helped me cope with the various circumstances I was confronted with, but it also contributed to a loss of memory as my body wasn't fully engaged in the whole experience.

The same feeling comes up when I sit down to write, and now I am seized with panic that I won't come back and will lose sense of this reality altogether for all time. Naturally, my head understands this won't happen because the conditions are entirely different, but my childlike heart is filled with intrepidation.

I call Namajira for support, "Dear friend, have you forgotten me? I would like to feel your presence once more. Will you come?" Breathing deeply and fully, I relax into my body, aware of my outside environment while tuning into my centre. With a single deep exhalation, a burst of golden light seeps into my consciousness and once again, I feel his warming presence.

"It be long time, has it not, my child? You be very busy this past year with your new mate, eh, what? You give me many laughs, taking life so seriously! Are you ready to play now?" Namajira slowly rubs his tummy and pats my knee at the same time. It is a funny gesture and reminds me of when I used to do that as a child, rubbing my stomach and trying to pat my head at the same time. I never could do it proficiently.

"Boy, am I ever!" I replied. "I've been so weighted down with the intensity of this relationship with my mate, I forgot to be light. How could I lose myself so entirely in this relationship when I had gotten so clear on who I was and how I wanted to be before I met him?"

"You want me to answer or you want to tell me what you discover?" Namajira mused, almost to himself.

"No, it's my story. I want to tell you what I learnt. But, oh where do I start?"

"At beginning, of course, child. You be forgetful again? Everything starts at beginning. Don't leave anything out. We all be waiting for this story!"

"First, let me tell you what the whales taught me."

Have compassion
for yourself
at all costs ...
for without this
you cannot
live with
passion

The wind was blowing, the air cool. I was standing at the top of a hill overlooking the water. It's the lagoon where the whales come to give birth to their babies and mate before travelling back up the north coast of America.

There was an eerie silence as I looked out on the horizon. Without warning, I heard a sound of rushing air and water and looked up to see a whale breaking the surface. Beside her swam her baby, mother and child synchronizing their movements so closely that it looked like one gigantic sea monster rising out of the water. I was struck with awe at the beauty and sounds that enveloped me as I reached into their water world and became one with the whale.

I am singing. I feel free and brave as I thrust my head straight up out of the water. I see a boat with people in it and they are looking at me, holding something up to their eyes, blocking a clear view of me, cameras. Are they frightened of me?

H. Sydney Salt

Why aren't they swimming like me? How restricted they look in their tiny boat as it bobs up and down on the waves that my mother and I generate with our tails. Do they know we are related? Mother tells me to be careful for they do not respect our ways and can hurt us. So the stories of the old ones go.

Once long ago, we swam free and without fear. Then big hard bodies called boats came along and dropped huge balls into the ocean. The balls tore apart our bodies and bombarded us with such harsh sounds that our minds exploded and we died in large groups. Those days are past, but we are still to be wary. The new people who see us seem to respect our ways and just come to be close and learn from us. We are the recorders of the earth story; touch us and you find more of your own history on this planet.

Slowly, I returned to my human consciousness and resonated with the truth of this awareness. I had gone down to Mexico with a small group of people to commune with the whales. I knew there was something for me to learn and it unfolded as I tapped into my own mental and emotional records of history. Not only of this lifetime, but many that I have lived before.

The record revealed was one of sacrifice. The

belief that I need to sacrifice my needs, my desires and my comfort for the needs and desires of others - for the tribe, the family. It is not true and does not support the evolution of the individual and ultimately the tribe, but it is a belief I've lived for a long time.

In my own family circle, I grew up believing that I was stronger than my brother. I was told that, emotionally and intellectually, I was better able to deal with life than he was, and because of this, I must always be ready to sacrifice what I wanted and give it to him. What sacrifice it was! From the smallest incidence to the largest catastrophy, the details unimportant now, I acted this part superbly. Little by little, I lost pieces of me, pieces that needed recognition of my worth and deservedness.

It is painful to see how many times I have acted out this martyrdom, not only for my own family, but for the larger family of brothers and sisters I encountered in my life.

What sadness this brings up for me. How much I lost of myself serving others needs and not my own. For with this belief goes the expectation that others will sacrifice for me in return. And they did not because they saw me as stronger. So I was left alone to fend for myself and I lost myself along the way. I didn't know how to access my desires, my dreams, because I lived for and through others. I helped them, gave them what I could and when they left, there was nothing left of me. I have done this with every relationship I have ever had from my mother and father, to my husband and child, and many friends along the way.

So this is what the whales encouraged me to reveal, my history of sacrifice. I learnt it was time to give first to myself, sustain my own way of being, and then reach out to support others. I was taught the opposite, as have many of us. I needed to see the history of our people, the pattern that I was now breaking free from.

Have no regrets ...
for you have grown from
those
experiences

as have
others.

8

I've come full circle now, but it hasn't been an easy journey over the last year. A man came into my life when I thought I didn't need anyone. He came to show me how I continued to believe in suffering and sacrificing myself to support others, and he helped me reenact my childhood experiences of abuse and escape through addictions.

I was intent on putting order in my life and feeling very good about the direction I was taking. I had decided to continue writing this story and, at the same time, pursue my vision of sharing my experiences and creating community with the outside world that I had left so long ago. What I didn't know was that I still had some healing to complete with regard to my childhood experiences, and this man was the one I had chosen to act out the drama I needed to expose and integrate it all.

Here, I must go back in my history to explain. During the last few years of my almost seventeen years of marriage, I began recovering memories of my childhood. Dreams, events and people began triggering memories that were both physically and emotionally painful for me to remember. These memories were locked and stored in different parts of my body and, as they surfaced, I found myself going deeper into the core of my being. I realize now, in retrospect, that it must have been quite frightening for my husband to witness such pain but I was compelled to go deeper to uncover it all.

As I peeled back the layers of protection, I became aware of how I slipped into different states of consciousness and could access memories of what appeared to be past lives, as well as this life experience. It became both an exciting and terrifying journey at the same time.

The memories in this life were about incidents in my childhood where I had been sexually and physically abused, not just by my father, but my brother, some of his friends and by my grandfather who sexually tortured me to "get the devil out." What was equally as damaging and abusive was the emotional and verbal judgements and criticism metered out by my mother and a society who denied my experiences by refusing to see my truth or accept my reality.

To this day, I have not had any of these

memories confirmed by members of my family, but it no longer matters. My withdrawal from men, especially my husband, and from society as well, were evidence enough for me that whether the incidents were physically real or not, they were real to me emotionally and psychically. I had felt profoundly violated and damaged.

As memories surfaced and I began to re-experience them emotionally, they slowly integrated into my being and became a part of my consciousness. I became less afraid, more truthful with my feelings. I stopped hiding behind my many masks of dishonesty and pretense. It felt good to take responsibility for what I was feeling, because I could finally attach it to its core experience and nothing hurt as much as that original one.

I saw that I blamed my husband for so much of my pain when he was simply acting as a catalyst to access that original pain. He was my partner to heal this aspect of my being. When I managed to get to the core, I was able to find compassion for the child who was misunderstood and suffered so much at the hands of her unconscious parents. And I was able to come into a place of love and gratitude for my partner for helping me reveal those many aspects of myself that needed healing.

I saw that what I remembered, I could make a conscious choice of action about. What I had forgotten, I unconsciously continued to pass on to others, especially those closest to me. I know this happened with both my parents. I now recognize that they loved me, but knew no other way, for their sensitivity and reality were not recognized and remembered either.

Throughout this time, I pushed my husband into revealing and healing his wounds. I knew instinctively that if he did not, I would reach a point where I would grow beyond him and I, somewhat selfishly, wanted him by my side. I know now that I was actually violating his being by pushing him into revealing his wounds before he was ready. I didn't want to lose this loving man. This man who should have been my father. He was kind and generous, accepting and honouring who I was, even though I continued to change rapidly in those last few years.

But it was not meant to be. For whatever reasons, his heart's desire was not mine. He had no wish to skin himself alive as he had witnessed me do so many times. I began to see that I could not complete my healing cycle unless he was willing to commit to a much deeper process for himself. He could not or would not. It doesn't matter now.

It was the saddest act I had ever committed, but I knew I had to leave. It broke my heart and his and I shall always have such deep regret for that. I had to set us both free because deep down, I knew we had finished our work and time together. He gave me my safe haven, my refuge to do my work, and I shall be grateful and always love him for that.

For almost two years, I continued to uncover more memories of hurt and betrayal of my spirit and grieved the loss of my partner, my husband. Then one day, a new partner pushed his way into my life and I embarked on yet another journey of rediscovery.

He was my wounded child incarnate and both the father and mother I had escaped from many years before. He came disguised as an educated man. Perhaps that sounds harsh, but I have come to believe that too much outside education gets in the way of our journey back to ourselves; that it is a barrier of protection against accessing our own individual history of pain. It keeps us in the mental realm instead of the experiential one.

I felt as though he used his education to further violate me and distance himself by not taking responsibility for his own reality.

At the time though, I didn't have enough confidence in my way of being and I stopped listening to me and believed his dreams and his truth more than my own. I began sacrificing my desires and budding dreams for his, because I didn't believe that I could live mine or make mine happen without someone by my side. I thought if I supported him first and what he wanted, then I would eventually get around to my desires and dreams. I began to believe his perceptions of how life was instead of tuning into my own reality. I believed his truth and, because it was different to mine, I felt I must have been wrong, that I must be lying to myself and others. I abandoned the lessons I learnt from the whales. I abandoned my spirit.

As I write this, once more I am overcome with emotion and confusion and I call to my spirit friend.

"Help me, Namajira. Help me understand this pain I am feeling. How can two people have two different stories and still be telling the truth? If I tell my truth does it mean that my mate is lying if our experiences don't coincide?"

"Dear child, I am here. There be mystery and magic in our world that we not meant to understand fully until we pass through experience.

So it be with relationships. Many times it be only after the experience we begin to piece together magic that took place." My sage friend spoke.

"I feel so ashamed, Namajira. I feel as though my very existence is in question when I am not believed. It is as though I cease to exist when my truth is not validated. Sometimes I feel that my whole life has been a dream. I'm not sure what is reality and what is not anymore. I listen to others and hear their truth, believe it, and then can't find mine. I'm not making much sense, am I?"

"It be alright. Sometimes need to babble - like stream, tumbling over rocks and reeds in its way - before we find truth. It is right to babble. Is cluttered mind emptying itself. Eventually, stream becomes clear as it runs course, just as your truth is illuminated through tumbling words and outward thoughts."

I felt calmed once more, by his lyrical words of wisdom and spoke aloud.

"What I do know, Namajira, is that it was time for me to find a way to bridge my inner world with others. To reach beyond my hurt and wounded self and extend my hand in compassion and love, especially to those whom I felt wounded me most. Sometimes I saw my pain reflected in my mate's eyes, but too often I just saw that he was hurting. And even though I knew it had little to do with me, I pulled back anyway and did not stand in my truth."

"What is hardest for me, Namajira, is to stay present with someone who is accusing me of something that I don't feel is true and not jump to my own defense. In this area, I was constantly challenged with my new mate."

"Perhaps it is because I was never believed as a child. No one stood up for me and took my side. I learnt that my very survival depended on me being able to defend myself from the many accusations that were thrown at me. I felt unprotected and vulnerable and fought for my right to exist and live without punishment or ridicule from others."

"And oh, how I was punished! Not only was I physically beaten, but I was locked away in my room for long periods at a time, sentenced to silence and isolation from the members of my family and the outside world. It was as though I didn't exist. Life went on outside my room, but I didn't know about it. All I knew was the silence, sometimes so deafening, I thought I would drown in my own thoughts coursing through my mind. I was afraid I was mad. I doubted my reality, my experience, because there was no one to witness it, no one to talk to, to listen to my story. No one knew my agony and despair of not knowing what was truth, whether I had been abandoned or that I really existed."

"Ah!" Namajira smiled, "so, this man came into your life to remind you of those childhood experiences. A time for you, once again, to remember what it felt like to be wounded child and feel attack from those who said they loved you. Ones who couldn't speak truth because of their own woundedness."

"Yes. I knew that it was time to re-integrate those parts of me that I had to lose in order to live in my world. And, looking back, I see that I would not get this experience with my sweet husband. I needed a more forceful partner."

"When I was a child, I had to give up my truth or risk losing my connection with my family altogether. I couldn't survive without them. So I buried my truth, my true self expression, and especially my needs and desires, in order to co-exist with them."

"At times, I didn't know where I began and my parents ended. They told me my truth. The boundaries were thin at best, and I wasn't allowed to create them for myself. I was afraid of losing the only caretakers I knew, just as I was afraid of losing this man. I began to believe that I could not exist without him and so sacrificed who I had become because I believed my very survival was at stake."

Namajira sighed, "Human relationship important way of learning, evolving, on Earth plane. One of human function is to serve one another, to bring into consciousness individual desires and needs through speaking our truthful reality. When we find this reality for ourselves, we begin weaving our history together with others to create intimate way of being."

I became silent for a long time, listening to the sounds around me, feeling sad and lonely once more. Outside the window it is drizzling. Everything looks green and fresh. I know I am on the brink of an exciting adventure, but all I can feel is sadness and regret for all that has gone on in my past. There is also fear in my heart for the unknown, moving out of my old behaviours into a new skin that I haven't clearly identified yet.

For many years now, I have held myself accountable for my intense array of feelings, and the actions I have taken because of those feelings. It has been a rewarding but, many times, very painful journey. It has been difficult coming to a place of compassion for myself and those who have hurt me over the years.

Voices In The Dreamtime

It has been more difficult setting boundaries with people I care about. I have tried very hard not to hurt others as I had been hurt, but that meant remembering all the many hurts I had experienced so that I could consciously make choices on my behaviour, to see where my intention lay. I know I hurt many people along the way, particularly when I chose what was right for me over someone else's feelings and well being. I felt I was abandoning them, rejecting them.

I finally spoke again, "I think what frustrated me the most with this man was that when I spoke my truth it became a battle ground for argument and defensiveness."

"Ah, but did you speak your truth or try to tell him his reality?" Namajira interjected softly. "There be violation of spirit! Person can only talk truth from their own experience. When you talk other person's reality, it not be truth but perception. This be not reality but judgements, pathway to non-responsibility of feelings and truth. When we judge others and do not take next step, we stop owning our truth, our reality."

"Well, what is the next step?" I asked, somewhat irritably.

"How well you know this, child! Next step from judgement is to see YOUR story, see what you saw in them, in you. Easy, yes?"

"No, it is not easy, Namajira. It is not easy to see myself when I see something I don't like in them. And it isn't the same thing in me."

"No, it is not. You must pick thread from fabric they weave, not entire cloth. It take courage, yes imagination, to see yourself in someone you not like. Great healing takes place when you own your ugliness and this be what your partner does for you - help you find shadow in you."

"I understand this, Namajira. I have gotten quite good at revealing my other half and taking responsibility for it.   The question I am struggling with is one of accountability, Namajira." I continued. "How do we hold others responsible for their shadow side and actions? How do we get them to reveal their inner feelings and take responsibility for them?   Do we have that right?"

Namajira turned to face me slowly. He looked deeply into my eyes before saying, "How can we not? It is why we here on Earth plane - define ourselves through others. I call this boomerang talk. We hold others accountable by speaking only our truth, not perception of theirs. If we do not speak our truth, it not give other person opportunity to make use of his free will to choose, take responsibility for his experience and speak his truth."

"If you know that you hurting person, do you want to continue?" He questioned. "Can you release person by talking your true feelings? A warrior risks death fighting for what he believe. So you must risk ego death to obtain mastery over your humaness, your woundedness. Only then can you come to place of alignment with one another. See your woundedness, respect your right to exist. Through your truth define your sacred expression of yourself, giving others chance to make same choice."

"Oh, so we hold others responsible and accountable by sharing our truth and giving them a chance to share theirs and letting them make choices for their conscious action? It is becoming aware of your true feelings and having the courage to reveal them. I see also that we need to set boundaries of how we want to be treated and then have to be willing to put those boundaries into action. So simple, and yet, so frightening to expose my vulnerability to others, Namajira; to trust others with my truth and hope that they won't hurt and betray me."

"Yes, child, especially with ones we love. But personal truth be one thing we respond to. We instinctively know when is truth, not mask of deception, as it comes with wave of strong emotion. As you be more truthful about yourself and your reality, so you see when others are truthful as well. If others cannot bridge with you and respond in this way, then like master warrior who knows he could conquer through sheer strength, you must walk away to find others with your strength of will and purpose. Do not waste precious energy using force for not their time. There are others waiting to link up with you and become part of your tribal circle where energetic path is of free flow and natural ease."

Namajira looks me in the eye and holding my hand continues. "Life not have to be struggle, you know. Challenge, yes. To find natural flow of life which carry you to your tribe, your Source. Many times you must stop, use your senses, for it be right in front of you. Life be about movement and stillness, when to do what. Listen to your truth, have courage to share it and act upon it."

"It was hard, Namajira, with this man because I thought I had already confronted my experiences as a child with my parents, but somehow, we created an environment to re-enact those intense feelings all over again."

"Yes, dear one, you had done lot of work on your own toward healing those wounded child parts of you, but you either need parents to recreate your reality for deeper healing or invite new partner to act them out with you. When you chose to lose memories of bad things, you think you cut them out, but they still be there, waiting to have light shed on them at appropriate and safe time. As a child you alone fought your battle, defended your truth. You did not have tools or others to support and sustain the battle, although you tried. You had to escape, leave it behind until a time could be found where you were on even ground. In your case, parents not willing to finish what they started with you, so you had to create partner to help you finish circle of wholeness."

"That makes sense to me." I smiled, "By the time I came to America, I had lost all memories of my childhood and created myself into a strong and willful person. I had hidden away the wounded victim-child I was. The man I married was the man I believed I deserved to have, gentle, giving and respectful. Together we created what I thought was a full life. It was only after our daughter's birth that I began realizing that there was a depth of feeling missing from our lives. I was only living half of my being. I had to find the other half of me or I would always feel incomplete."

"Yes and when you revealed your past, what

then?" Namajira asks.

"He couldn't respond by sharing his pain and somehow I felt that I was terribly flawed and ugly in his eyes. Here I was revealing my deepest wounds and all he could do was listen. Somehow I felt judged and betrayed. I saw that our marriage was based on living only one side of our personalities, the happy, 'I've got it altogether' side but there was so much more oozing out of me. I wanted to know I was not alone; that he too, had experiences that had hardened his heart, creating facades to protect his loving spirit. I wanted to be intimate on all levels."

"It's ironic with my second mate that I got to act out the sad, grief-stricken side of my spirit, but this mate, while willing to mentally grasp his own pain, instead wanted to keep it at the surface level and blame me for his pain rather than going to his deeper, intimate core. Very definitely a re-enactment of life with my family, with feelings flying around and no one willing to take responsibility for them. It was like living in a combat zone and not knowing where the next shot was coming from. When I revealed myself it gave them an easy target to shoot, and so it was with this man. Well, Namajira, please tell me I've finished my lessons with this last mate!"

"Let us see, child. Time will reveal itself!" He replied sagely, half chuckling to himself.

"Oh Namajira, that's not funny. I don't want to hear that. Thanks a lot!" joining in his now open laughter.

Love yourself as
no other ...
for only
you
understand
who you
really are!

9

I hear the sound of an ancient drum beat and feel myself being drawn into a vortex of wind and sound. As usual, my fear is great, but I feel compelled to surrender to the whirling circles I see vaguely before me. Suddenly, I am popped into a beautiful garden, serene and wild simultaneously.

I see a little girl squatting on the ground. She is dressed in a faded, yellow dress with a dirt-stained pinafore. She is shifting the earth around, feeling the texture as it runs through her fingers, marveling at the smell and colour of it. Scooping it in her hand, she puts the earth up to her ear and listens. A slow smile spreads across her inquisitive little face as she opens her hand to reveal a wriggly worm. Suddenly, she bursts into giggles as it tickles her hand to be free. She gently lays it down on the ground, watching it slither away into the earth.

I feel her absorption in the task she has undertaken. Nothing else matters. The world she enters is the only one that exists and nothing distracts her from being fully present with all her senses. There is no aspect of time, just a savouring of each moment as it unfolds before her.

How long it has been since I lost myself in my senses so openly and freely. How hard I have worked to get it back. For tied within those sensory experiences is my passion for life, for living. I call it my heartfire and that little girl holds the key.

Once again, my attention is drawn to that little girl. Out of the corner of my eyes, I see a young boy enter the garden. At first, he just watches her. Slowly he saunters over, pretending nonchalance, and squats beside her. He too becomes absorbed, but it is in watching her. I am saddened, knowing what comes next.

He begins to dig in the dirt in front of him and starts piling the earth into different mounds. Soon he, too, is absorbed in his task, but continues to glance at the little girl from time to time. He stops, looks around and begins pulling the earth away where the little girl is digging. At first, she doesn't notice and then, in outrage, she lashes out and strikes him on the shoulder knocking him off his haunches onto the ground.

I take a deep breath, fearing the inevitability of the boy jumping up and fighting her back, and because of his strength and size, overcoming her.

But wait, this is different. Something is happening that I've not witnessed before. There is a glint of respect in his eyes as he sits back up and calmly goes back to his own dirt piles, sifting the earth slowly and deliberately between his fingers, just like the little girl was doing.

"What is happening, Namajira?" I whisper as I call him into my presence. I am confused. Something magical just occurred and it's slipping past my consciousness. I want to grasp it before it disappears and is lost to me forever. "This is not my reality, at least, it hasn't been my experience."

"You see past as it is now present. This be way it was supposed to have been for you and wasn't. The little girl doesn't have to continue fighting for her rights. Just once does she exert herself and it is so."

"What am I seeing, Namajira? Is that little girl me?"

"Yes, of course. Girl you always were. Difference now be cast of characters you created around your life. Where once no one listen or hear your cries of outrage, now they hear and respond. It is right. That girl very passionate about living, don't you think? She speaks very clearly, using her whole body, not just her mouth. She has gained strength to respond with conviction.

She know who she is, what hurts her and what she want. You see your history as was meant to be in simple terms."

"Can life really be that simple? To give yourself up to the fullness of the moment? To respond spontaneously to the stimulus given you by defining yourself?" I query.

"Perhaps."

"I'm not sure I understand, Namajira. It doesn't sound grand enough. Surely, there is more."

"There be more always, child. But you must let it unfold as it happen. Too long you live inside your head, figuring it all out and missing truly passionate moments of your life. You live outside your life, not in it for fear of being hurt. You get hurt anyway. There always be cuts and bruises when you dive into action, but rewards are great and long lasting, for you live your life with your heartfire."

"But my heartfire got me burned in the past. Why should I trust it again?"

"Because heartfire was wild and free, out of control. Now it be channeled and focused. You use it to destroy, to cleanse, or keep you warm. Choice is yours. In big picture it be all the same anyhow."

I sighed. How tired I was of fighting my

imaginary demons in my massive mental head. It was time to let go of the fight and surrender to my senses. I realized that I was living a different life now. Where once I had to fight for my right to be heard, let alone protected, I now felt an almost tangible ray of light and love surrounding my every movement. There is little doubt left that I am guided and loved. Somehow, when I need something, it is provided. I just haven't learnt to fully recognize the signs and the giant shift in my reality.

"Namajira, it was hard leaving this last relationship. With him, I learnt how easily I sacrificed my boundaries, and what I knew to be true for me, to make him love me and stay by my side. I believe we were ultimately healing our relationships with our parents, he with his mother, and me with my father. I loved my dad so much and as a child, I did what children do best, give of ourselves wholly and without reservation. It was my dad's lack of boundaries that caused me such pain and it was my lack of boundaries that caused me such pain in this relationship. This is what he taught me. This man eventually showed me, that as an adult, I needed to set boundaries to show my love and respect for myself. It was a harsh and difficult lesson."

"But you learn, right?"

"Yes, Namajira, through it all, I learnt to love another as I had not loved since I was a child. Despite the fighting and invasion of my emotional and physical boundaries, I found my capacity to love again and for that love to transcend my hurt and pain. I am very grateful."

Honour your
self expression
in
everything
you feel, do and say ...
for this is
the way
to creation.

10

"Can you feel it? I can!
It is as tangible to me,
*   as a hit in the face.*
That's what it feels like,
A wall of unacceptability.
Someone doesn't like the way I express myself
And it is responded to by silence.

I hate the silence.
For within it, I feel judged,
*   condemned to death.*
A death sentence of isolation and barreness.
I am alone, and alone, and alone!
Always alone.

How could I do something,
*   or say something*
that incurs such hatred of my very being?
*   I don't understand.*

I am paralyzed.
I try to run away,
But I am held in place,
Transfixed by the unaccountability
  of this wall of silence
And the people who inflict it upon me.
Can you feel it? I can!"

I was reciting an old poem to Namajira that I had written at a time when I was just becoming aware of my relationship with my mother. Unlike my relationship with my father, where I was unable to have emotional and physical boundaries, my mother locked me out so effectively that I grew up believing that I was so bad that I didn't deserve to live, let alone take my place in the family circle of life and have a voice in that family."

"I have come a long way, Namajira," I whisper to him, my voice cracked with longing and sadness for all that I wanted and never had.

No more do I hear the chilling absence of sound. No more do I search for the lost unacceptable parts of me. It is all here inside me. I am amazed at the transformation that has taken place in my life. An old life filled with self hatred and fear of being loved, to a new life filled with anticipation and appreciation for who I am.

And yet, I am still unsure of each day and what it holds for me. I know it is about uncovering more of my heartfire, bringing my passion for living to life, but it still feels unfamiliar, strange.

"You know, Namajira, it feels uncomfortable to sit in a place of non conflict. The other day, for the first time, I consciously recognized that my anger was a mask I wore to cover my fear. It seems funny that I never understood this before. I've been learning what a powerful energy my anger is to access. You were the one who taught me that it was the doorway to other unexposed feelings, particularly to the hurt and pain I tried to cover up."

"Do not forget most important aspect of anger, to show your passion and desire to live," interrupted Namajira.

"Yes, yes," I said impatiently. "But, Namajira, I had not realized I accessed my anger to cover up my fear. What a great revelation this has been to me! Can I share my latest discovery with you?"

"Yes, of course. My ears are here for you. Know you not this, by now? Do you still doubt I am present within you?"

"I keep forgeting. So many times, I feel disconnected from people that I feel I must be disconnected from you, also. I know now that you are part of my spirit. That I lived as you, so many years ago when the white man encroached on sacred land. I understand more clearly that you have come into my consciousness to lend your personal traits of leadership and compassion, experienced from that lifetime. It's just that sometimes I buy into the old belief system that everything is separate and there is no connectedness of spirit. It is my humaness and woundedness born out of not just this lifetime, but many others as well."

"Yes! Been necessary to separate yourself from others and claim them outside yourself, just as you had to do with your personal experiences in this lifetime. Too much to cope with. In reclaiming each memory, each belief as separate, you come to identify the two parts of the whole and so begin the integration process. For you know, that be why you be born into this lifetime. The Earth planet and its people are integrating all systems into whole to evolve onto next plane of existence. You must continue to claim and own apparent opposites of all experiences to come to place of oneness," he reveals to me.

"Well, Namajira, I have not wanted to access and own all my fears. Some, yes, but not all. It has not served me in the past to show fear to those people who aggressively attacked me. My mask of anger was my protection, my weapon, so I could defend myself. Not just against others, but from myself. I was afraid to feel my fear of being hurt and ultimately, the death of my spirit."

"Show me what you mean, child."

"It's about woman's spirit and it concerns my mother, Namajira. She is dying. I think she has been wanting to die all her life. Now she is challenged once again. First with Alzheimer's disease and, most recently, with breast cancer. I suppose my wish for her is to die with dignity, but it seems, as has happened all her life, she is being robbed of this, too."

"Her life was a painful one. I don't think I consciously recognized that until recently. I want to honour her dying by acknowledging her life and what she gave me."

"Our mother/child bond began in the womb and has not severed, in spite of the physical and emotional wrenchings the relationship has endured throughout our lifetime. I believe that her conscious and unconscious beliefs imprinted themselves in my being when she carried me in her womb and were re-enforced as she continued to act them out during my childhood years."

"It was my mother's silence that I wrote the

poem about. There was fear and anger in that silence. It was from her that I felt isolated, judged. Yet, as I say this, I am aware in some twisted way, that she was trying to teach me not to be a victim. She didn't want me to live the life she had endured, one of isolation, criticism and denial of her individual and creative spirit. Ironic that the very experiences she wanted to protect me from were the experiences she, personally, inflicted upon me," I glanced at Namajira, and continued.

"I think she was disappointed about life by the time I came into her world. Perhaps, she saw in me a symbol of renewed hope, a way of leaving her mark in the world by teaching me how to live in this world, something that she didn't feel she achieved gracefully herself."

"My view of my mother is that she was unhappy, depressed. There was an overwhelming sense of sadness and oppression that followed her. A wisp of gray cloud that became a piece of her clothing, like a scarf, strangling her spontaneous, natural energy. I knew she wasn't always like this. I had seen photographs of her when she looked fresh, excited. Her eyes sparkling, as they reached out to the photographer as he or she happily snapped away. This was a vivacious and vibrant young woman."

I paused thinking about this photo in my mind's eye.

"Where did she go, Namajira? What happens to a woman's spirit when she gets married and begins her family? In my mother, what little spark was left was replaced by discontent. I've seen it in other women, too. They become part of a different program. A program that speaks first of sacrifice, a giving over of our needs and desires to the marriage partnership, and then to the children. My mother tried to give me many things that she didn't receive from her mother. But slowly the depression crept in and the sense of unfulfillment that she had sought first through her husband and then through her children, became overwhelming. She was overwhelmed at her inability to achieve success in a world she had set up for herself."

"I've wanted to know if the depression occurred because she felt she had no choices to express herself. Did she feel trapped and oppressed by the very life that she tried to create and stabilize through her children? As I look back on this period of our lives, I must own that the invisible child in me felt somehow superior to my mother. I saw that she was depressed and many times overwhelmed by the simplest tasks. I remember scorning her inability to cope and resolved that I would not be like her. I would make sure that I had lots of choices in life, that I would be happy and capable of dealing with life. What I didn't realize was that she was experiencing one of life's many emotions and passages. That eventually, given time and support, she would pass out of this particular life lesson into the next."

"But she was not supported to believe in her abilities to ride these waves of depression and hopelessness as a temporary state. She was not encouraged to express her deepest feelings. Certainly, it was not acceptable to feel angry. Instead everyone around her began to do the work for her, further disempowering her and re-enforcing her belief that she was incapable of dealing with life. It became a self fulfilling prophecy. And this is the legacy she passed on to me."

Namajira nudged my elbow, grunting, "Do you see parallel here? Your people deal this very same way with many lost souls without tribe or home. Can be temporary stage in person's life. But they be disempowered further by others doing things for them. Better instead to create circumstances to feel useful and worthwhile again."

"You mean people who are homeless? Yes, I see this. Must we go through these stages of development? It seems that these feelings of depression, grief and shame are in everyone at some point in their lives. Is it just women or do men experience expressions of oppression and worthlessness, too? Namajira, what pulls us out of it?"

"Anger be the key, as well you know. Tis the penetrator energy which moves us out of these deep crevasses of our mind. Darkness must be penetrated to get to lighter, subtle states of consciousness like love and acceptance. But first you must experience dark to know you are in it, you understand? Anger at being victim pulls you out, but must be on your timing, not someone else's."

I thought how sad that it was not understood in my mother's time that emotions are the catalyst for conscious choice. This particular rite of passage, depression, repressed rage, was only a stage to pass through. Instead it became an addiction, a way of life that she couldn't escape which she, in turn, passed on to me by not allowing me my natural expression and full range of emotions and desires.

With my mother's dying, I see that with her is dying my belief that I am flawed and broken, in need of being fixed. I see that she was taught the four S's. She lived through suffering, sacrifice, struggle and scarcity and wanted me to enact these beliefs about living also. It must have frightened her to watch my different stages of emotional development unfold and be expressed through me. As a child, I fought for my right to live my life differently. On some level I knew I had the ability and will to change my life by embracing all things, all emotions, as being part of the whole, not by judging and separating one from the other, labeling them to be good or bad.

Now I know there are developmental stages that we, as spiritual beings in these human bodies, must experience. From these circumstances, we grow and evolve before coming to the realization that we do have choices and our lives are, indeed, guided by a deeper knowing. But for a large part of my life I did re-enact my mother's beliefs and, in a way, it feels uncomfortable letting go of these ways that were so familiar to me. Playing the victor didn't feel authentic yet, because I played the victim role almost as well as my mother.

With all that said, I felt a deep sense of peace and acceptance finally wash over me. "Thank you, Namajira for your presence. I am glad that these parts of my mother are dying in me. The four S's no longer serve me. I am certain that my life is meant to tip the balance into experiencing the goodness, beauty, abundance and love for all of life expressing itself as God consciousness. I am so grateful knowing you are listening, knowing that you are me ... that we are one and always have been."

Have no
comparisons ...
for
    you
        are
    unique in
your own right.

11

As I sit in the silence of my being, I feel energy flowing through my body like a mountain stream. I feel alive with inner movement. I feel gratitude for the path I have chosen in this lifetime and for the many people who have graced my inner and outer worlds.

I draw great comfort in having Namajira to talk to. In the most intimate way, I have been disconnected from my own divinity, my greater consciousness. I accessed Namajira outside myself so that I had someone to talk to, someone who would listen when no one else would. In a way, he is my sanity. As I continue to tune in to my larger consciousness, there is so much I want to say and share. I'm afraid there will be no one to say it to. With Namajira, I am not alone and separate.

I think I'm finally getting it. I see that as humans on this planet, we divided and separated everything into halves, seeming opposites. We have done this so that we can act out both sides of the whole experience, whatever it is, whether it is good and evil, light and dark, emotions and intellect, chaos and structure. What we don't claim inside ourselves becomes a physical reality in our outside world.

Every emotion must be experienced so that we have an integration of our spirit - not disintegration - which is what most of us do in order to survive our world. As children, we are taught that while some emotions are acceptable, others are not. As we evolve into adulthood, we learn to cut off most of our unacceptable feelings. When I do this I am, in reality, saying that this part of me does not exist, that I do not exist. So I see all around me the manifestation of that which I refuse to believe exists within me and integrate in to my being. I see people acting out, on my behalf, the disowned parts of my selves.

It all exists. Because we refuse to acknowledge and own these parts of us, it becomes bigger than life and becomes life itself in other people. I am in awe of this system we have created, for I do believe that we have created it. This existence on earth is a world of dualities, a place to discover and experience, first a dis-integration of our spiritual being and then, hopefully, a coming together of our wholeness.

We do this by integrating the various parts of ourselves as manifested through other people that touch our lives and, indeed, all living things.

I remember my experience with Namajira at the fire circle when one man said "first we must separate to come together." It makes sense now. I saw it in such simple terms then. I have seen myself in so many other people, special people, who came into my life to show those parts of me that I dis-integrated from my being because of the traumas of my childhood. I came into this life to learn about and heal many parts of the soul, my soul and the collective soul. The lessons of judgement, acceptance, trust, faith, boundaries, creativity, compassion, fear, passion, service, truth and - the essence that encompasses and transforms it all - love.

I see my journey as one of practicing all that I have re-integrated through self-love. This is where the essence of my spirit resides, loving myself enough to take responsibility for all that I feel, all that I do and all that I believe, expressing it in a way that fulfills me and honours all living things.

By far the most profound realization for me is how I separated my divinity, my god-consciousness from myself. By looking outside myself to religious figures like Jesus, Buddah, and

Krishna for answers, I failed to realize my own divinity. These spiritual men show us our own divinity. We are not necessarily supposed to follow their teachings, but follow their example of accessing their divinity. They show us it is possible.

In the past I wanted to believe that wisdom was outside me in the form of great philosophers, teachers and even, doctors. I have witnessed the phenomena of people "channeling" wise souls no longer in their physical forms. I have come to understand that many of them are channeling their own divine wisdom, their god-consciousness. We as humans want to make life dramatic so we put this wisdom outside ourselves in the form of spirit entities. It is all part of our own divinity. Those wise souls that we want to keep as separate from ourselves are examples of our own power. Ultimately, we are all one. To recognize this divine power within us, waiting to be cultivated and nourished by our own integrated spirit, is to return home.

I am so awestruck by the simplicity of this that I want to somehow make it more dramatic. But if I did this, I would be continuing the myth and belief that we humans have perpetuated for centuries, that it must be dramatic in order to be real or true.

I am aware of a tremendous belief in me that the more dramatic I make things, the more I feel alive. I've observed this with my relationships with others. I believed that relationships were about sacrificing my needs and desires, suffering for others. Many of the recognized religions seem to support this stance. I acted this out many times, in different relationships, but I see it now as my love of drama which confirmed my very existence. Even though many times, it was confirming my existence as a victim, this was my role of unconscious choice because I was unwilling to clearly see myself as a victim or that I had a choice in playing that role. I was more attached to the intense feelings of drama than I was in taking responsibility for doing something about it. Perhaps because it did not evoke as much drama of sympathy and attention from others.

Consciously, I didn't want to see all the ways that I had fallen prey to life's many experiences. I wanted to identify with the victorious survivor, the one who fought her way out of many traumatic experiences. No, I didn't want to consciously own the person in me who was the martyr. That was too painful and embarrassing. After all, it showed everyone, including me, that I wasn't perfect, otherwise I would never have gotten caught in that unfortunate circumstance in the first place. The judge in me playing his old tape of "you should have known better."

The truth is that I have been addicted to the drama in my life, believing in struggle - and therefore, suffering and sacrifice - because it made me feel alive.

And if I let go of this belief, this drama... what is the alternative? Is it simplicity, beauty, peace? I confess that at this stage in my life, I don't have a strong relationship with this side of the duality but I am certainly willing to act it out. Heaven knows, I've done a lifetime of acting out the drama. Peace of mind, body and heart seems like a great alternative.

Be joyful and
live
without fear ...
for this
is
your natural
state.

12

It is late in the morning. The sun is shining brightly and I hear many small birds outside my window as I write. For the past few weeks I've been struggling with feelings of being lost and a pervading sense of failure as I have been reviewing my life. I'm aware that I am closing yet another chapter and moving into another level of existence. I am not at all comfortable with it because I don't know what "it" is.

My sense of failure stems from the fact that I do not see a physical way to manifest all the emotional and spiritual work that I have done. Perhaps, it is my harsh judge who is once again, telling me that whatever I've done it's not enough, that I have to be somebody special and different from my true self. I certainly don't see it as dramatic enough, especially since I don't have an identity recognized by the outside world. We live in a world where everything is labeled, who people are, is distinguished by their job, title or credential.

In the past, I have felt clearly identified in my roles of business-woman, wife, and mother. But I want recognition for what I have done with my life in recent years, yet I haven't found my title. Perhaps, I don't feel qualified to announce who I am to the world at large. I've called myself a teacher, healer, speaker and writer. But I haven't been able to make a living supporting myself doing any of these things. So I feel what I am most of all, is a pretender, a failure. Trying on these different identities, fitting them all and yet none at all.

So where do I fit in this physical world where we are judged by the job we have, the material things we acquire, what we look like? These are the measures of success. We don't get recognized or paid for "being." This is a world of human "doing"; of achievements and monetary recognition. Just like a flower is given fleeting appreciation and value, so too is a human "being."

My feelings of being lost emanate from my realization that I am, once again, letting go of my need for identity in the spiritual world. Yet, at the same time I want to embrace an identity that is recognized by my peers, in this physical world. This time, hopefully, it is without the drama of my belief in suffering and sacrifice.

"Why so serious, child?" Namajira seeps into

my consciousness.

"Because its hard figuring out what I'm supposed to do."

"Ah, so you still attached to drama of suffering, eh?

"Maybe. But aren't I supposed to do something significant with all the work I've done on myself? Surely, it's not enough just to 'be' for me?"

"Surely," Namajira mimicked.

"You don't understand, Namajira. I want to share what I know and get recognition for it in monetary terms because that is what the physical world is all about," I cried.

"So, it not be important enough just for you?"

"Yes... no, that's part of it. Going deeper into relationship with myself has been my identity for the past fourteen years. I want it to manifest in a way that others can relate to as well as benefit from my experience. I suppose I want to be rewarded in financial terms for all my work. Yes, I know I've received reward on a spiritual level, but Namajira, I live in a physical world. I must balance my spiritual life and rewards with physical, tangible results. Isn't this one of the reasons I'm on this physical plane of existence, to integrate the physical and spiritual parts of myself?"

"Yes, you are right," he pondered and was silent. He then said, "Perhaps you not see how spirit works and you try to make it happen your way, yes? Let go of drama of suffering and sacrifice, yes, but embrace drama of playfulness and pleasure. Stop trying to figure it all out, invite in mystery and magic! This be where you find passion... your heartfire, dear one. You work so hard at life, you forgot how to play with life."

Once more I reflected on his words. I think I've taken life too seriously for too long. There was a time I took nothing seriously and for the past few years I've been taking everything seriously. It is definitely time to lighten up and reintroduce myself to an old attitude I'd nearly forgotten... playfulness.

Speak the truth
at all times ...
for without the truth,
your relationships
are built on fabrication
without the framework
to survive

the
test
of time.

13

"Namajira, I want to talk about energy and detachment. You say it is time to bring back my sense of playfulness and yet, I find it hard when I feel someone close to me is wrestling with their emotions, saying one thing and doing another or when my head says one thing and my heart another."

"How so?"

"Lately, I've been noticing how people's words are vastly different from the energy they exude. Particularly with my most recent mate. He told me he wanted to have a committed, long term relationship and yet his energy and actions were clearly moving away from me. It took me some time to realize this because I didn't want to see that the words he was saying and his energy were in opposition to each other. I know now that he was not aware of this conflict within him, but I started reacting to his mixed message by distrusting his words and actions.

I would like to have been detached while this was going on, but I just felt frustrated because I couldn't quite understand what was happening when I tried to share my perceptions with him and our relationship became a verbal battle ground."

"I hear your frustration and sadness. Sifting through emotions to get to grain of truth be challenging with partner. There be much shame, yeh? You not have answers and want partner's help in understanding what be going on, right?"

"Yes, it helps to have a partner who owns his truth so that I can define what is going on for me. I hated not trusting him, yet I see that I had good reason. His energy and his subsequent actions were my confirmation. As long as I listened to his words, I couldn't detach and do what was right for me. I was reading his energy and felt incredible shame come up because I realized I didn't know what to do or how to articulate what I was feeling in response. I needed clarity from him in order for me to take appropriate action. I wanted us to define our individual truths and come into a place of action because of it. Is it wrong to want someone to partner you in defining your truth, Namajira?"

"No. But it means when both people tell truth, they might lose each other. That be big risk. Were you willing to hear his truth?"

"If he had said that he wanted to be free at the beginning of the relationship, I would have been able to make a clear choice of what I wanted. But no, as the relationship became more deeply entangled, I didn't want to hear that he wanted to be free. I would have felt rejected and our dreams together abandoned. As it was, I felt betrayed by his lack of honesty."

"But he needed you to define his truth. You both need to act out your parts. It be the human way. Most times that is only way we find truth, by doing. Had you been more trustful with yourself, you would not have stayed in relationship at all, yes?"

"Yes, I see that I didn't trust my perceptions of his energy and wanted to believe his words because they were what I wanted to hear. He simply told me what I wanted to hear. It was my lesson to trust my guiding voice for what I needed to do for me instead of listening to his words. I needed to follow my heart and instincts and not my head."

Namajira nodded sagely. "It be hard to tell truth to beloved because sometime, it means hurting them. You not realize that delay of truth brings greater pain later on when there is much invested in each other. Lot of puffed up expectations. You lay groundwork of truth, you survive test of time."

"But why is it that when we choose what is right for us, it hurts the other person?"

"Doesn't be so naturally. You look to another to fulfill your wants and desires, you always be disappointed. Person can't live up to your wishes, only theirs. Too much energy wasted in trying, always come to heart failure."

I suddenly saw why it was so hard to detach my feelings from my mate. I was looking to him to tell his inner truth and to fulfill my dreams. I had felt horribly betrayed when he didn't do either of these things. What a bitter pill to swallow. The little child in me still was not willing to grow up. I had just changed the form of mummy and daddy into my partner. Although I had grown up considerably in being able to take care of my needs, I was still attached to someone meeting my dreams and desires. He simply told me what I wanted to hear. Had I been putting my own energy into fulfilling and satisfying my dreams, I would not be attaching to his energy and what he needed to do for himself. We would both be free to pursue our paths individually...perhaps, side-by-side. Instead, we strangled each other with the demands we both made on each other. No wonder my heart felt so heavy.

Treat
yourself
with the
utmost
respect ...
your body, emotions,
mind and spirit ...
for these are your
gifts from
Mother/Father
Creator.

14

I am at peace. It feels a little strange. Yesterday I finished putting the words to some music I had composed some months previously and it feels as though I've entered another new level of acceptance within me. The song is simple and somewhat childlike, but it expresses my feelings of gratitude to my spirit essence, to the Great Spirit that weaves in and through all living things, the Mother/Father Creator.

Thank you for the time,
*   to heal my wounded heart.*
To find the peace within,
*   and bring me back to love.*

Thank you for the light,
*   within my darkest hour.*
You helped me find my breath,
*   to live my very best.*

H. Sydney Salt

Peace, light, love and laughter
  Are all within my grasp,
Gratitude and surrender
  Gave me back my precious heart.

Thank you for the sun,
  the moon and stars above.
The creatures on this earth,
  who helped to make me whole.

Thank you for my life,
  and all my blessed friends.
I live my life with grace,
  in ALL I see your face.

The reality of my life has literally turned upside-down and I see the magic of my journey more clearly each day. Perhaps coming from Australia to America was the physical metaphor I needed to complete this stage of my life. Every belief system I inherited from my family and the culture I grew up in has been questioned and re-experienced to find my truth. It couldn't have been accomplished without my Spirit essence always being present. There always a small child-voice inside believing in me, guiding me. This is the voice I chose to listen to when life became too much or when other people insisted on imposing their reality and beliefs on me.

It has not been easy. For years I felt inferior to my friends and family. They were educated and well read while I stumbled along, sifting through my experiences and beliefs. I was observing and interacting with my outside world while listening to my inner world. A world where nothing was solid or tangible, just a resonating energy within my body as confirmation of my truth. I didn't fit in. I felt judged and criticized. It hurt to be so alone and unaccepted for my way of seeing life and interpreting it. It worked for me, but so many of my friends and family felt threatened by me even though I didn't feel that I was imposing my way on them. I didn't understand that.

What I have come to realize is that every rejection has turned me toward a deeper and more rewarding relationship, not just with others, but with myself. My life experiences have become richer and fuller. I learnt to be grateful for this gift of redirection, although it was often painful. It always meant change.

There is a part of me that has wanted things to be constant in my life. I yearned for that feeling of security, knowing there were structures and people in this world that I could count on to be there, no matter what. Perhaps, that is why I was always examining my belief systems. I wanted life to be stable. Yet I saw that stability brought its own kind of poison; a rigidity of the mind, a stagnancy, and finally, the destruction of an inflexible system that ceased to grow and expand.

So I began embracing change. And with it, the realization that this is the natural order of life. There is a rhythm to every thing. From the seasons, to relationships, and to our own unique timing of the birth and death cycles within us. It is magical.

All I have to do is listen and surrender to the inner urgings of movement and desire. This, of course, has been a major challenge. How to tune in and access my desire; desire which had long since been subdued in me by society, friends and life experiences. Those in apparent authority who told me what was acceptable and what was not. People who imposed their systems on me in an effort to control or dominate, perhaps out of fear that their system would then be in question or not tolerated.

How easily I abandoned myself to be accepted, to fit in. How great the loss. For what I lost was the passion for my right, not just to exist, but to create a life that brought me peace and a happy sense of fulfillment.

For how can we be happy when we are living someone else's idea of life?

So on this day, I feel at peace. I am no longer struggling to be like everyone else, to fit into a system of someone else's design and timing. I am living this moment, knowing that it is precious and right for now. Knowing also that there is stability in change. I recognize that I am creating my day and therefore my happiness and fulfillment. I know that it will change, perhaps tomorrow or next month and that this is the natural order of things. I am glimpsing that I am happiest when I create something, anything. It can be the creation of my day, the creation of my environment or an artistic expression, like my new song. I am a creator!

"So, you think you have discovered the magic of life, dear child?" Namajira gently seeps into my consciousness.

"Oh, I think I am getting a clearer understanding of how life can work for me," I reply non-committally.

"How so?"

"I'm not sure I can articulate it in a way that makes sense to anyone except me. In simplistic terms, I sense that my intuition, which speaks from my whole body, is actually my Divine voice." I'm even a little scared to say that, in case I'm wrong.

"But, Namajira, I get a strong feeling that this intuitive voice has been the voice I've listened to all my life although I'm ashamed to say, not very consistently. Besides, there were a lot of other voices which kept me confused."

"I'm only just beginning to see how much I abandoned myself by brushing this voice aside. The thoughts that came up didn't make any sense in my real and practical world. But I see now that the voice was suggesting a path for my passion, my heartfire to express itself. It was actually leading me into a place of synchronicity and harmony with others. Does that make any sense?"

Nodding, Namajira expounded, "But certainly! You believed you ignored by God. It is you who leave God Spirit, you who chose not to listen to God-self."

"Yes, but I didn't know that the voice that was a part of me was also a part of God. I had been taught that God is outside me, in the heavens, not within me. Not that I am God. This sounds so blasphemous to my Christian upbringing."

"Indeed, it is! Now you not be so easily controlled by man-made system you call religion. You begin now to create sense of equality with others instead of creating ladder of superiority by those who must have power over others.

When you see, like wind, that breath of God blows through every living thing, you see wisdom that each flower, rock, tree, bird, and creature brings to you. But especially, you see you... divine you. Everything has place, everything in natural order." Namajira paused. "It is sad to see. Life on this planet so misunderstood. So little value given to divine rightness of all things. Yes, it be very sad!" He shook is head slowly.

"Well, where do we go from here? How do we change a system that has been in existence for thousands of years?"

Namajira's voice was silent. With simultaneous feelings of dread and excitement, I knew it was once again, time to enter another story of the dreamtime.

Listen to the voice
of reason,
respond to
the voice of
passion.

15

As I close my eyes, I hear the hum of electricity all around me. It is not frightening this time, but reassuring, as though the air is popping open. It feels like wires of bondage being whipped free from my body, the space around me expanding. There is nothing in my mind's eye and I sit still listening, feeling the energy, wondering what will happen next.

Nothing! I call to Namajira to make his presence known. Again, I am met with silence. What is happening? I'm beginning to feel uncomfortably, unsure of what I need to do. I don't like sitting in this open space anymore. The child in me is getting impatient and just a little scared. There is nothing to focus on, to draw upon, grab hold of. I'm sitting in a white void. I say white, because I have felt this void before, but it always felt black, as if there were things in the darkness waiting to be brought to light. This feels as though there is nothing there, just white space.

Is this my world of possibilities? Can I begin to create what I want out of this place of nothingness?

Suddenly, I am thrust into a scene. I am walking down a dirt path. There are trees on either side with poison ivy sprouting out of the ground in front of me. I know I must be careful so that I don't brush up against the ivy, but it is not difficult as long as I stay to the centre of the path. Off to my right, I hear water falling over rocks, gurgling, the sounds bouncing off the canyon walls. I have a strong sense that I need to follow this path to the end. Yet I am wondering how far that will be. I didn't come prepared. I am wearing a sun dress with open sandals and I didn't bring any water with me.

I am aware of the sounds surrounding me. The birds churping, a lizard scurrying across my path into the underbrush. I have a moment of panic as I imagine encountering a rattle snake sunning himself on a rock in front of me, blocking my path. The sound of the water grows more intense as I quicken my pace and, just as I round a bend in the path, I break out into an open space.

Before me is a magnificent sheet of water cascading into a crystal clear pool. My senses are reeling with the beauty before me and I catch my breath with the wonder of it all.

There are huge boulders scattered around the pool as it channels itself into a free flowing river tumbling over rocks and reeds in its way.

I want to get closer to the water, so I climb over the larger boulders looking for an easy way down to the water's edge. With a steady heart, I hop from rock to rock wending my way through the obstacle course that has been set before me. Finally, I drop to a granite slab closest to the water and plop down. The water is cool to my feet as I dip them into the pool. It is calming to me.

As I look around, I realize that I am alone. There is not a soul anywhere. It feels as though I've found my own secret garden. I am not afraid and I don't feel lonely. This is new for me. I am feeling deeply connected to myself and to my surroundings and I realize... I am not alone. There is simply the absence of other humans intruding into my world. The sounds become fuller, the smells richer, as I sink into the energy that is being provided for me.

I look up and see a hummingbird sitting on the branch of a tree. I don't think I've ever seen one sitting still. His wing feathers are green and under his throat is a beautiful irridescent red. As I focus on his beauty, he begins to sing. It is a high-pitched kissing sound.

He puffs out his chest and seems to know that I am admiring his being. His balance is a wonder to watch as the wind softly blows the branch he is perched on. He sways back and forth in the breeze with ease. I am joyfully aware of his gift of revealing himself to me.

I am reminded again of the hummingbird's unique maneuverability and his taste for the sweetness that life has to offer. I thank him for his message of lightness and being. It is a message that I want to hear and respond to more and more each day. To recognize that I am able to move into and through any challenge that is presented to me and to choose to see and live the sweetness that is offered by these situations.

"Yes, 'tis choice that makes difference," I hear as Namajira strides into view, his gentle presence warming my heart.

"Oh, Namajira, I thought I was alone and then I knew I wasn't, even though you weren't here. I felt a fullness that is new to me."

"Tell me, child, what have you discovered about yourself?"

"I think it is tied in with what you said about choice. Last week, I decided to go on my version of a vision quest. I wanted to spend time alone without any of my usual distractions, to see where my next step would take me. I had been feeling frustrated because I didn't know what to do. I felt I had a lot of choices, but nothing seemed to excite me," I paused. "You know, Namajira, it's strange not coming from a place of survival where you do whatever it takes. Knowing I am free to choose makes it much more difficult. I get overwhelmed."

Namajira nodded his head, not interrupting.

"Anyway, that was my dilemma and I was determined to find the answers on the trip away. My whole trip turned out to be about choices... Where did I want to go? Did I want to camp where there were no signs of human habitation or did I want to use campgrounds. Do I stay at a hotel instead and what hotel?"

"I finally chose to go to Mt. Shasta although I could find no logical reason. I just felt called. Does that make sense, Namajira?"

"No need to make sense, just feel right, yeh?

"Yes, it did. Finally! After I agonized over it for days. I wanted so much to be guided to do the right thing but I could find no guidance, just a flickering wish that flew by as fast as a hummingbird darts away. This was the theme of my trip. Trying to catch that illusive, fleeting desire which was followed by an overpowering voice of logic and practicality.

Which voice was I supposed to listen to? I was making myself miserable, when I finally stopped and asked myself why it was so hard for me to make choices."

"What did you find out, child?" Namajira asked kindly.

"Choosing meant loosing, Namajira. As I went back to my memories as a child, I saw that I was constantly being asked to choose either my mother or father. When I chose to be with one parent, I perceived that the other one felt hurt and rejected. The way they dealt with their feelings of rejection was by pulling away their love and physical presence. It felt awful! I became so conscious of hurting them that many times I didn't make a choice at all and then I lost any desire I had for what I wanted. Later, when I started dreaming again and began living the way I wanted, I felt I was hurting people with the choices I made. Many times I pulled back and did nothing."

"I thought by not acting on my desire, my choices, I could keep the people that I loved in my life and that they would not feel hurt by my actions." I fell silent, feeling the full impact of this belief and the grief surrounding this core choice I had made.

"Namajira?" I asked tentatively.

"Yes, dear one?"

"The fullness I am experiencing now has its essence in giving myself permission to make choices for me, regardless of how they will affect others. I don't mean that I now do things thoughtlessly, but I've stopped interpreting how others will respond to my actions. Also, I'm following my heartfire even though it doesn't have a reasonable or logical explanation. Too often I heard outer and inner voices tell me I had to have a 'good' reason for doing something and I felt effectively stopped. To do it just because I wanted to was something I rarely allowed myself.

"'Tis good you now be willing to take risk by choosing. It no longer be your reality to choose and lose."

"Yes, when I made choices I believed either I got hurt or I hurt others. Now I know that being hurt is not dependent on other people's reaction. And that I hurt myself more when I don't follow my heartfire or try to anticipate how others are going to react to me. I've been stopping my natural flow of energy because I was afraid to be alone and unloved."

"You, at last, love yourself more to fill yourself with heart's desire. Well done, child! You succeed in first lesson to create new world for yourself and others."

I stood up feeling exalted, the pool before me looking invitingly seductive. I wanted to strip off my clothes and dive deep, stretching my body into the clear water below me. I hesitated. I couldn't see the bottom. Maybe it wasn't safe to go in. Wait. I had choices. I could take a calculated risk. I slipped off my clothes and gently slid in, rejoicing in the newfound freedom of my spirit and body.

Respect your solitude
as an
intimate path to
self knowledge
and
regeneration.

16

Slowly opening my eyes, I see the textures of my physical world. Everything, so much more brilliant and sharply focused after my journey into the dreamtime. Where once it scared me to lose track of time and place, I now feel a growing confidence in my ability to come back and bridge the two worlds.

It has concerned me that I spend too much time alone. Yet I am happy. There have been times of intense loneliness where I yearned to be with somebody, anybody, just to fill that horrible hole. And I have been aware of using my friends to fill that gap of loneliness as well as to stimulate desire in me. More and more, I find myself choosing to fill my time inventing activities that interest me and bring me pleasure. In fact, I keep choosing time to develop my relationship with me.

There was a time when I felt that deepening my relationships with my friends, and having a partner, were the most important endeavours I could have. Yet, I see in that process, I neglected to really know me, except in the context of others. I think... I know, I was afraid to confront myself, to be alone with me for any extended period of time.

In recent years, I've had a lot of time to rediscover myself without the stimulation of friends or the many other distractions and addictions I've lost myself to. It's been quite a sobering experience.

I don't believe I truly realized how important this time was for me. I see more clearly now that I have been striving for deep intimacy with others when I didn't yet have it with myself. I inevitably ended up getting lost in many of my relationships. I didn't know what I really wanted out of me, only what I thought I wanted out of others. Was I now willing to support me the way I supported others in achieving their desires and dreams? Was I willing to access those parts of me that I had hidden from myself?

It seems that Spirit, mine and the collective whole, decided it was time. Just as I had helped others, I needed to be open to support and guidance from others. It was my fear of revealing myself and admitting that I didn't know all the answers that lead me through my addictions. I was afraid to be intimate with others. I didn't want them to see how truly confused and inept I felt or to feel the hurt of their judgement. In truth, I was more afraid to be intimate with me, to look at myself. I was afraid there was no substance to me or that I was so ugly no one could possibly love me or want to be with me. I certainly hadn't wanted to be with me, knowing the me I knew.

As I expose these words to my consciousness, I see, in my mind's eye, a scene.

I am looking at a deeply wooded area. The air is dank, smelling of wet leaves. The sun filters through the trees as I spy a cave about a hundred yards ahead of me. Out of the cave lumbers a large brown, grizzly bear. He is swatting at the ground and swaying back and forth. He is angry. He looks up at me and it seems as though he is scowling. I ask if he would be willing to communicate with me. He begins to talk.

"Why should I speak with you, woman? You have ignored me for so long. You have no value for my ways."

I started protesting, "But that's not true, I...." and fell silent at his glare. It was time to listen, not defend myself against perceived accusations. He continued.

"My way is simple. Yet you have refused to acknowledge me. I am furious for being ignored. It is as though I don't exist. You see my size.

My message is big, like me. How could you not see me, feel my presence within you?"

I had no answer for this massive beast. He was right in that he was large and powerful. What important facet of my life was I ignoring, something that was this large and powerful within me? I remained silent.

"Do you want to know what I bring to you?"

I nod my head, submissively.

"It is the gift of time alone; of sleep and hibernation. It was not so much that you did not do this, it is that you put so little value on it. You whined and complained because you wanted to be with others. You didn't respect or listen to your need to be alone and give yourself the luxury of reveling in this place of solitude. It is the place of healing, of regeneration and hope. It is the place of self-love, where you reveal yourself to you, giving yourself over to explore the inner caves of your being. I felt disrespected by your lack of enthusiasm."

With that, he faded from my view, leaving me alone with the truth of his words. I couldn't deny that I spent a lifetime running away from myself. I have been afraid to reveal and access what I wanted for me and although I came to realize the importance of it, I still resented it, too.

I called to Namajira.

"I need to talk, Namajira," I demanded, somewhat irritably.

"But of course, child. I am here."

"I'm feeling confused. I think I'm just beginning to realize that I have not experienced true intimacy with my friends and partners."

"How so?"

"I haven't been honest, I mean truly honest, with my communications with people. I thought it was because I was afraid that I would hurt their feelings. But I see now that in that action, I was interpreting that they couldn't handle my truth, and with it, perhaps, my rejection of them."

"That puts you in position of superiority, does it not? You make that decision for them. If you believed them equal, you would not take away opportunity for them to respond and grow."

"Yes, Namajira," my heart sank, "I feel so ashamed. I believed myself better able to handle life and disempowered them by not allowing their natural response. What I actually did was reject myself and whatever it was that I needed to do for me. And... I ended up resenting the other person for not speaking their truth."

"Yes, daughter, it be difficult to have the courage to say what you want, but price be very

145

high indeed if you do not. For relationship built on fabrication of lies and false expectations. These do not survive the test of time. The ultimate lie is you believe person cannot deal with choice of your desire, your honesty."

"Namajira, I have been brought up in a culture that says that it is good to put other people's feelings and needs before your own. I believed that I was protecting them from my selfish ways. I was supposed to compromise, but everytime I did, I lost a part of me. I didn't like the word compromise because it meant giving up what I wanted for the sake of what someone else wanted. But I got confused when I wanted to be with someone and yet we couldn't agree on what we could do together. I ended up sacrificing my needs for theirs and not telling them the truth of what I wanted. What am I supposed to do when this happens?"

Namajira grunted, "Two things. Reveal yourself to you first. Find your true desire. Then see what is most important, activity or being with this person. If it be person, start negotiation of possibilities. If it be activity, be prepared to go alone or with someone else who be in harmony with you at that time. Remember, it not be negotiation, but compromise, when someone loses.

Negotiation is where everyone wins but it takes longer. Sometime, courage needed to reveal choice to go alone."

"Gee, Namajira, I get tired just thinking about it. It requires conscious choices and honest communication to have healthy relationships, doesn't it?"

"Yes, that be so, but rewards be great. You find worthy partners to co-create a new way of living on earth planet. That be good way."

With that said, Namajira popped from my consciousness and I was left alone with a feeling of anticipation for what could be.

Savour the
present to find
the pleasure.

17

The day has just begun. I've woken up happy. No reason, just glad to be living the life I have. So grateful to be in this season of plenty, as Namajira would say. As I yawn and stretch, my mind scans through the activities I must do today and ponders over what I would like to do. The beach, that's where I want to be. Dare I do what I want over what I should do? Gathering my things together, I toss them into my car and head for the coast.

Once more I murmur words of gratitude that I live in a place where the sun shines brightly on the water only ten minutes from my home and that I have the freedom to choose how I like to spend my time. Arriving at the beach, I spread my chair and towel out feeling the pleasure of digging my toes in the sand and warming my body with the rays of the sun.

I breathe a sigh of relief that I am here, present in this very moment, feeling the sensuality of the day. As I close my eyes, I feel Namajira's wiry body sitting beside me drinking in the pleasurable moment as well. I see his body as a dark, black-brown, glistening with sweat, the droplets roll over his skin like broken beads of a necklace scattering in all directions. It's so beautiful to watch, everything in slow motion so that I can drink it all in.

"Do you think it's OK to be happy, Namajira?" Out of the corner of my eye, I see him raising one eyebrow.

"I don't think it was when I was growing up. I have memories of me singing at the dinner table and being asked to stop. I remember times of exuberance and being told to 'tone it down.' Someone was always interrupting my moment of pleasure and happiness, telling me I should be doing something other than what I was doing. What I perceived from these experiences was that it wasn't alright to be happy and to do things that brought me happiness. In fact, I was positively selfish for indulging in things that gave me pleasure. You know, Namajira, I haven't even tried to pursue happiness as I hear others do. I don't think I believed it was my right. How strange!"

I fell silent as I thought about all those times my parents and teachers unconsciously squashed my enthusiasm and dreaming. I remember the first time I saw a live play. It was *My Fair Lady.* I came out of that theatre dancing and singing, brisling with enthusiasm; swearing that "one day I would be on stage singing and acting the part of Eliza Doolittle." I recall vividly, my mother's response as she laughed and ridiculed the idea as an impractical and unworthy goal; not to mention my lack of talent as she perceived it. She didn't realize to a sensitive eight year old how devastating her words were to my ears.

Such an insignificant incident by itself, but one often repeated over the years when I voiced my enthusiasm to follow a dream. Eventually, I stopped speaking my desires out aloud for fear of ridicule and criticism from others and somewhere along the way, I stopped dreaming, even to myself.

As I look back, all of these dreams had to do with expressing myself creatively. I wonder why it frightened my mother so much and why she couldn't encourage it in me. How much happier would she have been if she had allowed herself to follow her dreams!

Beside me, Namajira begins softly humming to himself and I find myself caught up in the strange melody. As I listen, my throat begins to hum along in a totally unconscious way, weaving my own melody through his.   Without thought, words began forming into a chant as I tapped out a drum beat on my thigh.

> *"Dream, dream*
> *Find your heart's desire*
> *Live your life with fire*
> *Be your dream*
> *Share your dream,*
> *Now!"*

Namajira and I smile at each other as we drift into a warm and companionable silence.   Yes. I think its alright to be happy now.

Sing
the
songs
of silent
suffering ..
for grief is
necessary on
the path to
wholeness.

18

I am having a day of silence. I have two old and faded pictures in front of me. One is of my grandfather holding me as a baby, probably around the time I was eight months old; the other, a picture of my grandmother, standing above my mother who is kneeling above me, the baby. I am drawn to this second picture which shows an obvious link from generation to generation. I listen in the silence for more of the hidden message of what is contained in this brief glimpse into the past. I hear the voice of my grandmother say, "Silent suffering was the woman's place in our family. We could not break the bondage, but we are sending you our love and energy so that you can."

And so it was! It has been a journey of suffering and despair for the women in my family. But not just the women. It was the feminine spirit that has suffered and despaired of ever finding recognition and respect. I know now that I was the grief carrier in the family.

I expressed what they could not. I carried the stories they could not tell or allow themselves to feel. I am the storyteller of pain and suffering, hopes and dreams.   The voice of the child I was, speaks out:

> *"In the silent suffering*
> *I heard their pain and cried.*
> *I saw their Spirit, their beauty,*
> *when others could not.*
> *They showed me their pain*
> *by acting it out on me.*
> *I gladly took it on*
> *to bring them comfort and ease.*
> *It was the part of me*
> *who felt responsible for their sadness.*
> *I felt I needed to be like them*
> *to understand their pain.*
> *Yet, all the while my heart was crying*
> *with tears of joy,*
> *For I knew this was not my way to live."*

As an adult, I now see the tyranny of the old male spirit of mental and physical domination and control passed from generation to generation. Not only from father to son but, in my family, from grandfather to mother to me.

My mother carried the voice of judgement and oppression while my father could not hear his feminine "song."

I knew in my heart he was a gentle man, but he was conditioned to be so tough, so unyielding with others. Where did his gentle spirit go? I saw glimpses of it when we would speak of our dreams and question what life meant to us. I remember him being sympathic to my mother's pain. But what of his own? He couldn't allow himself this. So how could he really feel her pain? What a loss for us all.

Where was it written that men were not allowed to share their pain? Why was it alright to provoke war, but not alright to tell simple stories of their own emotional pain? Why did they have to wait until the pain became physical before they acknowledged that they were hurt? Were wars started so men could feel their pain, share their woundedness in an acceptable manner?

I saw my struggle fighting for this acceptance of letting my pain speak, to both my father and mother. Did they think I was so hideously scarred and flawed because I showed my woundedness, the vulnerable and emotional side. Or did they think that by witnessing my pain, they would then be accountable for the pain they felt and the pain they inflicted? Why was it weak to feel and strong to not?

I used to sing songs with my father, songs from the gentle island of Taveuni in the Fiji Islands where he grew up. He taught me to play the ukelele and together we would sing, harmonizing our voices. How precious those moments!

When my father lifted his head and sang, it brought tears to my eyes. I am so sad for the "songs" he felt he had to sing to others. The songs we sang were filled with love and gentleness, but the voice my father used to others was different. I knew my father because I knew his Spirit, but I only caught a glimpse of him through his music. The "song" he chose to sing to the world was harsh and cold, without feeling. I miss the tenderness he showed when he sang those island songs. I wanted to know him more, to break down his walls of protection and isolation. I sensed his deep self-hatred for not living up to himself... what he thought a man was supposed to be. He struggled with being a dreamer, a philosopher, an inventor and instead, having to be a provider.

I don't think my father wanted to be responsible for others, only himself. He wasn't allowed to, his family wouldn't let him, nor would his culture.

He had no one to share his burden of responsibilities, no one to help sort through the confusion and fears he felt. He was taught to be a man: "A man doesn't feel. If he does, he is weak. He can feel for others, but not for himself." But I didn't understand. How could he feel for others when he wasn't allowed to feel his own pain?

How I loved my father for sharing his tenderness with me. How sad I am that he kept going away, retreating emotionally and often disappearing physically. I think perhaps he felt he exposed too much of himself and began hating himself for being "weak", for not living up to his own expectations. He tried to control his world by running away so he wouldn't have to be responsible for the pain he felt and caused. Didn't he realize my pain was caused by him abandoning me? Everything else was endurable except this pain. He left me wondering what I had done wrong, floundering in confusion as to how I was to live my life.

There were no more songs to sing, no blending of our different voices. I liked our differences. I didn't want to lose him because he felt different. I wanted to celebrate our differences, to know him better. I felt robbed and sad that he chose to leave.

Was he really that unacceptable to himself? Yes, that song he taught me very well.

But I am truly my father's daughter. I am sensitive, sensual, an explorer and a dreamer. I dreamt of a gentler time and that time has come. My wisdom came through finding my feminine "song," recognizing my feelings and expressing them. With every experience, I am able to dive deeply into the hidden parts of my being to find my truth. To bring it up to the surface, feel it, speak it, trying not to be afraid of the responses from others or to expect certain results. Feeling the fear and not letting it hold me back.

There was a time when I was afraid that if my story was different than other people's then I wouldn't be able to connect with them. That if you couldn't relate to my story then we couldn't bond through the sharing of common experiences. Can we bond by being different, having different stories?

In tribal times every voice was heard, from the very young to the very old, male and female. It was only through this process that solutions and decisions were acted upon. It was the weaving of stories and opinions that counted, sometimes similiar, sometimes different, but each person remaining in constant connection with his or her individual truth.

I realize this has always been my passion, to speak my truth, to be heard and accepted for it. My song is one of freedom. Freedom to express myself my way, creating an environment of acceptance for others to tell their story, their way. There is no one way, there are many paths. Each path needing to be expressed to weave into this tapestry we call "life."

I'm beginning to accept that it was not only fear that held me back from staying connected to my story, it was shame. I almost lost my way because I took on my family's "song" of shame of the feminine spirit. I chose instead to be vulnerable, emotional, and not know all the answers. All my life I felt judged by others and then by my own inner judge. It expressed itself most clearly through the voice of my mother, my father too ashamed to allow his voice to be heard. I grew to believe that I was scarred, horribly unworthy, that no one could possibly accept, love or understand me.

But through it all I stayed in connection with that whispered voice urging me to believe in my experience despite outside voices of contradiction. It was the voice of Spirit, my Spirit and it called me home, to step inside myself and feel my wholeness, knowing I am truly well loved and whole.

Children are our
teachers, showing
us those parts
of us we deny
in ourselves.

19

So here I am this bright sunny morning, the air fresh after a heavy winter rain, feeling cleansed and whole. There is a fluid peace all around me and I marvel once more at the softness of my world. More and more I experience longer periods of peace. Have I changed that much? Or has the world around me changed? Perhaps it is both, but the most profound changes have come from within me.

As I consciously confront the opposing voices that arise, both within and without, I give myself permission to feel it all, not cut off or ignore part of my natural emotional response, pretending it doesn't exist. I now enter into each experience deeply and fully, using all four "bodies" of my being to integrate and heal the surface hurt and the deeper core underneath.

"My family didn't understand, Namajira, that everytime I stuffed down a feeling, it found a place within my body as a solid mass and accumulated with every other hurt that came along? I spent a lifetime depositing unwanted thoughts and feelings, holding them inside me. But everytime I did this I was cutting off a part of my very existence. I was learning to disintegrate my being, to compartmentalize my world into just two 'bodies', the body of mental reasoning and the body of physical reality. I was disconnecting from my spirit body by ignoring my emotional body!" I looked around for some visible sign of Namajira's presence. And I heard the fluid melody of his voice.

"Yea, spirit flow through every living cell. Whole body living intelligence, not just brain. You stop flow of emotions, you make unnatural dam. Much like rock placed in river, water learns to go around. Soon branches and rocks are pulled to it, becoming bigger, constricting flow. Water must find another path. So too, does ignored energy in our body draw to it more of same matter and constrict flow of spirit coursing through us. Energy find another path, but original block still there, building, waiting to burst into physical dis-ease because it has nowhere to go."

Namajira sighed. This was not the first time we had discussed this concept of physical disease resulting from unexpressed feelings accumulating in the body. It was ideas like this, and how I've used them in my healing, that Namajira urged me to write this book about; simple truths working in my life.

When I became challenged with my own physical illness, I started to see things from a different perspective. I saw that by the time it became physical, the stuck energy was releasing through my body and that I had already begun the healing process. This was a good thing. Through listening to the physical expression of my body, I began my journey back. I then allowed my emotions a voice and mentally reconnected each painful memory associated with a hurt in my life.

When I stayed fully present, allowing my physical, mental and emotional bodies to express simultaneously, I noticed another energy coursing through my body. I came to identify this force as my spirit flowing freely, healing and integrating my being on a deep cellular level. The emotional expression helped identify and release my spiritual body. It was the spiritual body that was the integration point.

I see more clearly than before that my middle years were about re-integrating the many selves that I had split off in order to cope with my many dramas.

Because I had been conditioned to believe that many deep emotions were not to be revealed, I cut off most of them and kept my expressions at a physical or mental level of understanding.

I think we gain knowledge about ourselves by remembering our feelings. But most of us only experience this knowledge on a mental level - to make sense out of it, therefore it remains simply knowledge. When we are willing to bring our story to life, experiencing it fully through our whole body, connecting our emotions to spirit, we attain a deeper knowing, This transcends knowledge into wisdom. Then we speak with passion, born out of our own wisdom, alive with spirit expressing itself through us.

This then has been my passion, integrating my many selves utilizing all four bodies of my being. I had to get to the root cause of my illness, my unacknowledged spirit.

I knew that the conflict outside me could only be resolved by addressing the conflict within me. I had to recognize that my sexuality, and how I expressed myself, my creative side, had been wounded and that it was inhibiting me from living in peaceful co-existence with others. I had to listen to the voices of judgement about myself and others and pay attention to each voice, accommodating them into my being to obtain peace.

From this, I began to come to terms with my greatest fear. When I am freely expressing, as a child does, experiencing all four bodies at one time, the physical, emotional, mental and spiritual, I am at my most vulnerable self. My history of attack, punishment and ridicule, from those who professed to love me, had kept me in fear of expressing my essence in its raw, creative state, much like I did as a young child. And yet, it is this vulnerability I yearn for. I don't want barriers of protection, masks of facades, to keep me from connecting fully with others. I want that expression of openness and vulnerability reciprocated because, it is on this deep level, I feel no separation of spirit from myself or to another.

Until I reclaimed my original wounds, I didn't have the information to recognize violation much less set boundaries. I had learnt that it was painful to express my emotions openly, sharing how I feel and asking for what I want. Yet I also learnt that it created a depth of intimacy that soothed my soul and filled my heart. I am willing now to risk that more every day.

Perhaps it was learning a different way of perceiving the roles of perpetrator and victim. Was the victim strong, the perpetrator weak?

Pondering this thought, I ask for Namajira's input.

"I think neither. We experience both parts of our being to integrate, dear one. If you only play one role you must find other actor to play opposite. Better to realize that we play both roles at different times, then integration come. Look at our world, many people playing roles of victim in different parts of world. Yes, it is so. Also, many others play role of perpetrator. Just look at war zones around planet to see this. In world of opposites, as earth planet is, we humans must play both sides before we have integration. Sometime, we take many lifetimes to do this. It be no accident, all part of big design. It be larger picture of smaller one. World be replicate of you. So you must play victim and you must play aggressor to return to wholeness. Tis good, yes? Life is fair then. Victim and perpetrator role neither good nor bad, all for greater good of humanity, becoming victory for single soul, you!"

It made sense. It was hard for me to show my victim or vulnerable side, because it encouraged more victimization, but when I learnt the role of the aggressor, I balanced out the energy, becoming victor over my own experience and pushing back the attack.

For me, both roles have brought me much shame. It was this shame that held me back from intimacy with others. I didn't want to reveal those raw parts of me, I wanted to pretend I was perfect. But I'm not, and when I share my imperfections I realize I am not alone. Others carry their scars and when we share our stories, we feel less isolated, more connected to each other.

Most of us carry the pain of abandonment and have felt the grief of rejection, isolation and betrayal. Feelings of being less than, not fitting in, and not deserving, are shared by most of us, but we keep it secret, not daring to reveal those intimate parts of ourselves for fear of further isolation and pain.

I thought I was afraid to die. I thought I was afraid of change. What I was most afraid of, because of my wounded sexuality, was intimacy. Showing to others, once more, those parts of me that are less than, what our culture tells us must be, perfect. This is my greatest challenge and I suppose it is for others as well. We have all been wounded and scarred by our life experiences because we were open and vulnerable. Can we risk it again, knowing that to do so could bring us the opposite of our original experiences. By revealing our Ab-original selves, our primitive essence, could we find that we are no longer alone and instead find joy in the recognition of our true oneness of spirit?

It is already happening in my life as I see it in many others. It is the letting go of our fear of intimacy that is finally uniting us as a people and this is my most fervent wish.

Reveal the
    feminine
essence
    to
    heal
    the
        masculine
            spirit.

20

It feels today that I am most afraid of living my victory. If only I am willing to risk ego death once more, and drop the shame of my woundedness in order to embrace my victory of recovery. This is where I face my unity with others.

It is through the sacred expression of ritual and storytelling where I feel safe and most connected. And where I journey, once more into the dreamtime.

. . . . . .

I'm standing with Namajira at the crest of a rolling hill, mists swirling gently through the valley stretched before us. I hear singing, but I can't see anything through the mists. I look to Namajira for confirmation of the voices I hear and he smiles wistfully.

"It be woman's time," he said briefly.

I look at him, questioning with my eyes but

he says nothing more. I am drawn to the voices. I want to explore what's going on. I tug at his arm and we gingerly edge, one step at a time, down the hill toward the sounds. I sense Namajira is holding back, but I'm not letting him, as I continue to lead down the unmarked path. Now I clearly hear women chanting, harmonizing their voices, each one seeming to sing different words in different keys and yet, all sounding the same. The sound is other-wordly.

> *"One step, I take with you in my mind.*
> *One breath, I make with you in my heart.*
> *One soul unfolds, surrounded by love.*
> *One step, one breath, one love."*

Stepping further down the hill, we arrive in a natural amphitheatre formed by the valley floor. Namajira pulls me to face him.

"I only go this far. You must walk alone now. They be waiting for you," gruffly he pulled me to him in an awkward hug, letting me go abruptly. Suddenly unsure of himself, he smiles shyly, saying, "I be glad we come this far together. Do not forget me. We join up later."

I look up at him slightly puzzled by his words and actions, knowing he won't explain further. I smile tentatively and turn to face the path before me. The ground beneath my bare feet is soft and damp, the grass cushioning my steps, as I walk soundlessly to, what I now perceive as, a circle of stones surrounding the base of this sacred place. The mists look like soft swirls of whispered wind painting a mystical effect around the scene before me. Within the mists many women are dancing in two concentric circles facing each other. Drawing closer I see they are clothed in a rainbow of flowing robes, a dance of colours, ethereal and earthly at the same time, all blurring into one.

I am being pulled into the magic of the circle as I fill my body with the celestial sounds of blended voices singing to and through me.

I am home! This is where I belong, within this circle of women! As my body affirms this realization with tears of joy and grief, the outer circle parts, inviting me in. At first I am hesitant, asking myself how I could possibly be a part of this circle of magnificent women. Yet my heart sobs with the recogition of this truth.

With gentle reverence, I am passed from woman to woman spiraling slowly toward the center. As I pass each woman, I am stroked and cradled gently in her arms. I am being birthed! I am overcome with emotions, surrendering at last to the sweet softness of this moment.

My rational mind has left me. I am deep within the vortex of energy created by these midwives of light and love. I am placed in the centre of this sacred circle as the women welcome me through song and movement, each creating her own unique dance of invitation and acceptance.

How I have longed to be welcomed into this family of women. It is something my mother could not do, nor her mother before her. I needed to know I was part of a sisterhood. I wanted to be acknowledged as one who could contribute to and be a part of a community. I needed to know I was valued for the individual way a woman, me, expresses her being. I had grown up in a man's world, feeling isolated and alone. Although I didn't know it, I yearned to come home to the feminine path, a path of effortless movement and timelessness, following the energy of the heart, not the head. Yes, I am home here.

Slowly, gracefully, their voices drift into silence and all outward movement ceases. I am cradled in the arms of Great Spirit, protected, welcomed, accepted and loved. I revel in the sounds of spirit, letting it fill me entirely.

A soft breeze brushes my face and I look up to see the women creating a tight circle around me.

A tall, robust-looking woman speaks out, "You have done well, child! The journey has not always been easy, but you have triumphed over the many obstacles put in your way. Your journey was to explore abandonment, by your God Source, your culture, your family and your own sweet spirit. The challenges along the way led you to believe you had little value. You chose not to show your full self. Instead you diminished yourself, to you and others, to fit in and be accepted, believing only in your undeserving of fulfillment, connection and love."

Another woman spoke. She was small and dainty in stature, yet her voice was deep and full. "You continued to perpetuate this myth by concealing your beauty, intelligence and talents. Yet you tried to balance your feelings of inadequancy by supporting others to shine. This was your apprenticeship and you did it well."

One more woman stepped forward to say, "Finally, on this night, you stopped pretending that you are less than others. We see your willingness to take your rightful place on this planet. We hear your voice. You have birthed yourself one more time and we here acknowledge and support you for it. Welcome home, dear woman."

I listened in amazement as tears of relief

flooded my face. It was true. Almost from the time I was born, my memories were of not being wanted, perhaps, even resented. I never felt I belonged. I felt odd, different. No matter how hard I tried, I didn't fit in like everyone else appeared to do. Yet here in this circle, I knew there was nothing I need say or do to be accepted. My mere presence was enough, yet I knew my voice would be heard if I chose to use it.

"Nothing is wasted, all is accounted for!" pipes up a young pixie-like girl. "It is good to know that every word, every breath has value for someone. Thought forms become real when believed. Be careful what you think!" she warned.

My heart skips a beat as I acknowledge these words. Yet I ask myself, are we creators of our individual and collective experiences? Time has taught me that this is so, but it has been a difficult concept to reconcile. I had to ask myself the most difficult question... did I create my original abuse?

· · · · · ·

As my own healer, I had to gather every ounce of compassion and acceptance for the child I once was. I had to believe that she was a victim of her environment and culture. I had to know that her verbal, sexual, emotional and physical abuses were beyond her control and were not caused by her behaviour, but by the lack of responsibility of the unconscious adults around her.

I saw that I had inherited a lot of beliefs about myself and others through these interactions as a child. As a young adult, I was unwilling to own my woundedness, playing the role of tough survivor, but the unclaimed energy was that of a victim... of forgotten childhood hurts.

I was stuck in a role I didn't even know I was acting out because I wore the facade of survivor. But the belief systems were already in place, with the voices of judgement and condemnation shadowing my every action and interaction. Voices that spoke of blame, "you asked for this, it's your fault, you made me do it, what's wrong with you?" and an even smaller voice responding "I must be bad, I'm not good enough. Maybe they'll love me if I do everything they say. I don't understand. What did I do wrong?" It was these voices that held me back from expressing myself more fully and pulled me away from living my life with passion.

By my mid-thirties, I finally created the internal safety and external support to examine these beliefs and sort through the experiences interpreted by the child. I believe I now create the life I lead because of the thorough commitment I made to uncover my Ab-Original self.

I do create what I believe about myself and the world that surrounds me. Did I create the original abuse? I choose to believe that while I did not create my exact life circumstances, believing these were co-created as my life unfolded, I did have an original plan before my birth to learn certain lessons, first setting the scene with my family of origin and then connecting with others in my greater family, to heal and grow from these original experiences.

I sense that I've come to this Earth many times, playing many different roles to evolve my being. I believe that, just like a play, there is a large cast of characters that have chosen each other to individually and collectively play specific parts for our personal evolvement, time after time.

I think that the Earth environment is one of duality of spirit. A place where everything has been fragmented in order to be examined and then integrated back to its wholeness through the recognition and playing of each part.

I believe that what we are all seeking is our "home" and that while we catch glimpses of it throughout our lives, coming home is going back to spirit, to the original One Source, many people call

God. I believe that, as a people, we share this abandonment of our own spirit and our belief of the greater abandonment of the God Source because of our cultural concepts of the God role.

I don't think this God Source is a negative force as I was taught, but rather a neutral, creative force allowing us as souls, in physical form as well as spirit, to co-create at will.

I believe that we, as humans, do have choices and it is whether we are making them consciously or unconsciously that decides the quality of our journey back home.

I am glad to have arrived at this point in my life where I am in full recognition of the roles my core family and greater family have played in my life. I see them all as precious gifts for my own unfoldment and I am filled with gratitude and awe.

I know now that I do not walk alone and that my greatest teachers were my most harsh. Perhaps, had I not put on so much armour over the years, I might have heard their message more easily, but this was also part of the grand design. I am aware that being more conscious does not make me exempt from further learning, it just makes the walk along my path more graceful.

There are many families where I have felt

welcomed and many where I did not. As long as I kept returning to myself, I was never alone. I was given many gifts, the greatest of which is my imagination. Without this, I would never have dared to dream and enter the dreamtime. It is here that my soul is found, whole and intact.

· · · · · ·

Turning my attention back to the sacred sisterhood, I breathe deeply, relaxing my bodies into the present. The women have drawn closer to me as four women step forward. The ritual begins.

Each woman is given a cup filled with water.

One woman holds it high above her head saying, "This water symbolizes the fluid movement of all things... our emotions, our blood, our spirits, nourishing all life."

"It is so!" we say and each drink from the cup.

Another woman steps forward, scooping up a handful of dirt, "With this earth, I acknowledge the Great Mother who gives us the foundation and knowledge to regenerate our lives, sustaining us with her bountiful gifts."

"It is so!" as we each in turn, scoop a handful of dirt, letting it run through our fingers to return to the earth.

"I pay respect to the air, blowing it's winds of change; the breath of new beginnings and the death of old structures." So says the third woman.

"It is so!" we say, breathing in deeply the breath of life.

And the fourth woman steps forward, holding a torch aloft. "With this torch I ignite the element of fire, symbolizing passion, the life-blood that illuminates and transforms all in its path."

As the torch is passed, each woman stands in its light as she verbally affirms her passion for living at this time in her life, allowing herself to fully bathe in the light of the fire.

I hear my passions spoken over and over again as each woman speaks...."peace, love, unity, compassion, solitude, communion, freedom, healing, respect, gratitude, surrender, laughter, music, dance, song, silence, fulfillment, harmony, diversity, acceptance, service..... wholeness...."

The silence that follows is deafening, the air pregnant with the seeds planted in the wind. The intention is set.

And so it is... the promise of now. Not something to be acted upon in the future, but to be immersed in the action of now. Women of spirit, women of the earth.

Conscious
integration
of every voice
illuminates the
soul.

21

Slowly the mists clear and I am alone sitting in the center of the circle of stones. It is the dawn of a new day. I hear birds churping all around me, singing their morning song of welcome. It feels good to be alive!

There have been many times when I gave thought to leaving this planet, but something always held me here. Perhaps, I instinctively knew my path would be a long one. There was always a feeling of destiny to be lived out and I had only to find the road. I didn't realize that I was already living my destiny. It wasn't something down the road, in the future, it was living life fully in the present moment, trusting myself to move with the urges and instincts that bubbled to the surface of my consciousness.

I didn't trust the journey, thinking there was something else I was supposed to be doing. I had been conditioned to look ahead, escape what was present or live it fleetingly with an eye toward the future.   I was programmed to think with my head... "be rational, logical," not allow my sexual-creative urge to lead my heart.

It was the child who was most connected to her spirit, but I learnt that I wasn't supposed to listen to her.   Adults were my role models and there were few who listened to me. I didn't know it was their experiences and resultant fears, their lack of nurturing that held me captive in my own body. Their layers of protection became mine as I added my own interpretation of new experiences in ever-increasing layers of oppression.

My path had to double back to pick up the lost pieces of my natural development, lost because I had to fragment my spirit in order to survive. But it's not a matter of survival anymore, it's a matter of thriving, flourishing in the richness of my experiences.   For I have discovered it enhances others lives, just as I have always wanted to do, when I am able to share my stories. It has been my shame that has held me back. It has taken me this long to realize that the shame I carried was of those who were unwilling or perhaps, unable to travel their personal road to recovery yet.

"Could be, it be your destiny to lead the way now, dear child," Namajira pokes into my consciousness abruptly.

"Each person hears different drum beat. There be many people to lead the way home. You must do your part."

I sigh, affirming this thought to myself. Namajira continued, "Remember how you make snake rattle? It was symbol of shedding skins of protection to find your Ab-Original self, yeh? We carry many people inside ourselves at different times in life. You had to find boy and girl child to find spirit essence of yourself. Children held key to imagination which led you to self knowledge. Your whole child spirit be broken for long time. Girl hidden, boy numbed."

Namajira paused, smiling, "It be your boy spirit who held key."

"My boy spirit!" I exclaimed. "What do you mean? I thought it was the little girl in me who was so wounded?"

"May be girl in physical form hurt, but mostly divine children be in hiding. This spirit always intact. I not talk about physical body of you as girl/woman or boy/man, but soul energy of boy and girl inside you. Soul essence always there, whole and complete. We call it divine feminine, meaning energy of ideas and creation not yet formed. You be given plenty of those, yeh? Always imagining!" Namajira smiles.

"Little girl very connected to her source. Then protection put on because of attacks. She stop trusting her knowing and not let boy do his job. Your boy spirit hid away, afraid to move. He was the one who made ideas and creation happen. You get it now?"

"I think so," I said slowly, trying to sort out the words to interpret the pictures that had formed in my head. "Are you saying that whether we are in the body of a male or a female, there are two greater energies living within us and you are defining them as boy and girl spirit, divine essence?"

"Yes, that be so. It is how I see it, anyway. When all is not allowed to exist and work together, it become bigger struggle to live. Much like a clock, each part be different, but essential. If one part not working, other parts must make extra effort - not efficient, clock may not work at all. Same with humans," Namajira paused to see if I was digesting this information and waited for my thoughts.

"I see that. Then, in my healing process, I needed to first find my femaleness, remembering those feelings that had been injured or not allowed, like my tears of grief, pain, and anger. I see that I was protecting the emotional energies of the feminine.

I couldn't allow the boy/male essence in me to express them because whenever 'he' did, I was beaten, punished, isolated or abandoned. It was the boy spirit in me that was so wounded, the one who was to manifest the feminine energy... the emotions and ideas of creation."

"Namajira! I wonder whether that is why I am here on this planet at this time! Have I come to do my part in healing the male spirit by intergrating it with the divine feminine? I thought it was to heal the feminine, but I see now that she was just concealed. I had to bring her out in the open, trusting and acknowledging her wisdom so that I could begin to heal the male side of my being. What a thought!"

"It be true. For eons male spirit be abandoned and disconnected from his feminine counterpart. It be through the feminine side that he be reunited with his spirit. Otherwise, life continue to be big struggle, male spirit always feeling needy and incomplete, cutting off big chunks of himself to survive and not knowing why he feel so lost and alone. Major destruction of himself through mutilation and war, outside and inside his body. No matter whether you be in female body or male, feelings still the same, results still same.

Finding your feminine reunite you to divine source, and through her, male can manifest highest ideals."

Namajira fell silent as I tried to digest all that we had said. There was something eluding me as I kept going over in my head what we had just spoken about.

Softly, with a whisper caressing my ears he said, "Know you not by now, I be your male spirit?" He paused, looking deeply into my eyes. "You disconnected me, putting me outside yourself so you could reclaim, through ritual at circles, those feminine parts of you that be lost and hidden. Now I be ready when you are to walk hand in hand, creating life the way you want... with beauty, in balance and peace. Let us merge together, being not male or female, but divine essence expressing itself as love for humanity and all life."

And so it is!

* * * * * *

MY STORY

I was born in the land Down Under. Growing up in Australia taught me about isolation and resourcefulness; coming to America brought me freedom and integration.

Over the years I've worked in radio and television, marketing and promotions, taught advertising and published articles for a variety of magazines while completing numerous studies in writing, psychology, philosophy, religion, intuitive sciences and shamanism.

Through my work with the Girl Scouts of America, developing and teaching leadership skills, communication and responsibility, I reconnected with the "bush child" of Australia, which brought me back to the Earth and the rediscovery of my "Aboriginal" heritage as well as the American Natives' philosophies of my adopted land.

With the totality of my life experiences, I began teaching Creative Awareness Workshops, bringing magic and meaning to people's lives through the exploration and integration of their inner world. Using storytelling, music and ritual, I now create workshops, retreats and events to help people find community and wholeness by the rediscovery and healing of their creative and spiritual natures.

My life today is a work in progress sharing this book and encouraging others to see where they fit in the Tribal Circle of Life by supporting individual self expression and the creation of their personal vision and dreams.